How to SPEAK TV

A Self-
Defense
Manual
When
You're
the
News

HOW TO SPEAK TV

by
Clarence
Jones

Copyright © 1983 by Clarence Jones

Cover and type designed by:

Kukar & Company, Inc., Publishers
3490 S. Dixie Highway
Miami, FL 33133

ISBN 0-914603-00-0

First printing September, 1983

Printed in the United States of America

Table of Contents

Preface

The first time you face a TV news camera, it is like standing before a firing squad as they load and slam the bolts forward.

Ready **You feel naked.** It seems the whole world is watching, listening.

Your mind races, trying to form your last words. Words that will live after they fire.

Aim **You sweat.** You keep your hands out of sight. They shake. Your mouth goes dry. You hear yourself stuttering. Before the words are out, you wish you'd said it differently.

Why this panic? You've done nothing wrong. Yet you feel guilty. Clumsy. Cornered.

Fire This kid asking the questions, pushing, jabbing, seems to think of himself as a bush leaguer destined for "60 Minutes." There he goes again, twisting what you just said. His smirk says you're lying.

THIS IS NOT FAIR! you want to scream.

But you can't.

For 35 years, television reporters have been conning or cornering people to play this traumatic game: **Interview Poker.**

"I don't know how to play," the interview target gamely says.

"That's all right," the reporter smiles, "I'll explain the rules to you as we go along."

This book is designed to teach you the rules, and some of the basics of television news. Hopefully, it will make the odds more even, the game more fair.

Television speaks another language.

When you see the broadcast version of the interview, you may wonder if the person on-screen is someone else impersonating you.

While the camera was rolling, if you were able to control your panic, you thought you were straightforward, concise – maybe even witty and well organized.

But when you gather your friends and family to watch your debut on the six o'clock news, you look evasive, long winded, downright stupid.

Each Day, 10,000 TV Interviews

Every day in the United States, more than 10,000 people are interviewed for television news. Most of them are unhappy with the results. If you work in government or law enforcement or certain types of high-profile industries, you know the feeling.

If you're a corporate executive, educator, lawyer, hospital administrator or union official, sooner or later, you'll be talking to a television camera. Chances are, you won't have any warning or time to prepare for that conversation or confrontation.

If you ever expect to be interviewed for TV...if you need to get your message to the public...if you want to be an effective spokesman...if you expect to be quoted accurately and fairly...you MUST learn the language of television news.

There's no great mystery to it. TV news stories follow simple formulas and techniques. Most of the time – believe it or not – the reporters aren't trying to make you look bad.

But if you don't understand how to speak Television, they must pick from the few usable phrases you scatter through your conversation. They didn't quote you out of context. They used the only sentence you spoke that was understandable. The rest – for television news – was pure gibberish.

To communicate – to defend yourself, your client, your organization – you must learn how to play the game. **How To Speak TV.**

Chapter 1

For the End of the World, Two Minutes

Time dictates almost everything in television news. Newspapers have deadlines, but they can be stretched. If a major story is breaking, the press run can be delayed another 15 or 20 minutes—sometimes more.

Television deadlines are absolute. The news begins at exactly six o'clock, or ten, or eleven. The lead story must be ready when the anchor says, "Good evening." Sure, you could place that story 15 or 20 minutes later in the newscast. But if the audience is expecting today's big story (they heard about it first on radio) and it's not ready at the top of the newscast, they'll switch to the competition.

A newspaper reporter can write the story long, with the less important facts at the bottom. A makeup editor will chop off the last paragraphs if they don't fit.

Time restricts television stories in two different ways. The producer—who assembles the newscast—must design an exact 30- or 60-minute newscast. Each story is assigned its amount of time early in the afternoon. If the story comes out of the edit booth 45 seconds too long, then the producer will have to find 45 seconds that can be dumped somewhere else in the show. Once the story is edited on videotape, the length can't be changed without a major overhaul effort. There isn't time.

The 17-Minute Newscast

Time is absolute, and it is precious. After you subtract commercials, weather, sports, good evening and goodbye, a 30-minute newscast is only about 17 minutes of news. Most stories will run 30 seconds, or less. A few will have the luxury of a full minute. For a major story—90 seconds.

Producers have an inside joke they scream

when young reporters say they need more time for a story. "What do you think you're covering?" they yell. "This story is worth 90 seconds. For the end of the world, two minutes. But only if it's really good."

Walter Cronkite once said television provides a headline service. Newspaper people love that quote. For much of television coverage, Cronkite was right. But there are other times when neither the written nor the spoken word can come close to the awesome impact of the television news camera and microphone.

Television has unified us more than any other force in history. The storytellers in ancient tribes gave people their sense of time and place and identity. Then books served that purpose. Now, some of those moments captured by television bind us together as a people. More powerful than books, they are engraved in our collective memory. So much so that we sometimes have to think a minute — did I see it on television, or was I really there?

- Jack Ruby killing Lee Harvey Oswald.

- The rescue of survivors after the Air Florida plane crashed into the icy Potomac.

- Helicopters being pushed into the sea from the aircraft carrier as Saigon fell.

- Martin Luther King speaking at the Lincoln Memorial.

- The launch of a space shot, or the first step onto the lunar surface.

- The shooting of Robert Kennedy, and George Wallace, and Ronald Reagan.

For those stories, television forgot about time. When it does, and when luck and skill put a camera in just the right place, no other medium can compare with it.

Day-to-day newscasts are another matter.

Television has radically altered the way most Americans receive and retain information. Thirty years ago, first graders had an average attention span of 20 or 30 seconds. Today, that is the limit for most adults. Television's ability to flick from one picture to another — sometimes several times per second — has conditioned us to *expect* frequent changes of scenery on the tube. When it does not happen, our attention begins to drift.

Television stations and networks hire consulting firms to study viewers — to learn what turns them on, and what makes them switch to another channel.

Thou Shalt Not Exceed 90 Seconds

It was those consulting firms that issued the 90-second Commandment. Sure, the commandment is broken. But unless it is exceptionally well done, any story longer than 90 seconds tends to make viewers yawn, get up to go to the kitchen, the bathroom, or to bed.

Or worse — switch stations.

Those same studies led to another time commandment: Never let anybody talk on camera for more than about 20 seconds. The voice can continue, but you *must* constantly give viewers new video. If you want to retain or improve your audience ratings, change the picture more often.

Network news has whittled down considerably that time edict for interviews. When you watch the news tonight, time the interviews. They will probably run about ten seconds.

How can you possibly say anything about a complicated, controversial subject in ten seconds or less?

It is a skill that can be learned, no more difficult than driving a car or playing bridge. The fear of doing it wrong, of embarrassment and public ridicule, the fear of being badly used or abused by the reporter makes talking to television seem so terribly difficult.

Understanding what television news needs and how it must assemble its stories will take away some of the fear. And, like driving a car or playing bridge or public speaking, the more you do it, the easier it becomes.

Later, we'll give you exercises to develop mental agility for boiling down complicated subjects. How to get to the point quickly. If you expect to communicate effectively on television, it is a skill you MUST learn.

But first, you need to understand some of the story forms. You can't fill in a crossword puzzle until you know how long the space is, what comes before, and what goes after.

Attention Spans Set Story Forms

Many of the story forms for television news are dictated by attention-span requirements. That's why the double or triple anchor format was invented. If viewers begin to nod, the new face and voice brings them back to attention. Many local stations believe male-female anchor teams offer maximum appeal and attention-span advantages. The anchors are usually attractive people, easy to look at and listen to. The shift back and forth between male and female voices offers constant attention fresheners. If they're not listening closely, men in the audience enjoy looking at a beautiful woman. Female viewers like to watch a good-looking anchorman. And the chemistry between a man and a woman on camera makes ad-libs more interesting.

The Anchor Balancing Act

Television stations balance their anchor teams in the same way a political party tries to balance its ticket. A city with a large black population needs black anchors. Stations with significant ethnic communities search for anchors who've lost their accents, but have identifiable ethnic names and *look* Spanish, or Italian, or Polish.

Television amplifies monotony. Fifteen seconds of a lifeless voice seems like forever. Broadcasters train themselves to read so their voices go up and down, now slower, then faster without a breath, before a long pause.

In putting together a newscast, the producer tries to pace the show the same way. A long story (90 seconds) will be followed by several short ones. The plane crash report may be played just before a break. When they come back from the commercial, there will be a fluffy, breezy story to make you feel better.

Copy Stories

The simplest and briefest television story is called a "copy story" or "reader." The anchor reads the entire story, on camera, with no visual effects. It is usually no longer than 15 or 20 seconds.

Keys

To make a copy story more visually interesting, a graphic of some kind is "keyed" in the upper corner, over the anchor's shoulder. The graphic is inserted electronically, in the control room. You know, of course, the drawing, or picture, is not actually there in the TV studio. If it's a story about a postal workers' strike, there may be a postage stamp, or a mailbox in the "key." A copy story about a murder may "key" a gun, or a knife.

TelePrompTers

While we're talking about copy stories, you may wonder how anchors read the news without looking at the script in their hands – and why they bother to have it there.

The latest TelePrompTer devices enable anchors to read stories while looking directly into the camera lens.

This is what the anchor sees when he looks into the studio camera lens.

The TelePrompTer operator feeds script sheets to a conveyor belt that passes under a closed-circuit TV camera.

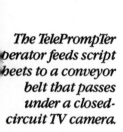

The pages are actually on a small conveyor belt, across the studio, out of sight. A tiny, closed-circuit television camera is mounted over the conveyor belt.

The TelePrompTer monitor is reflected by an angled sheet of glass in front of the camera lens.

On top of – or under – the big studio camera, a black-and-white TV set receives the picture of the pages on the conveyor belt.

7

The picture is reflected onto a plate of clear glass in front of the studio camera lens. The angle of the glass is fixed so the anchor can see the reflection of the pages, but the camera can't. In fact, the anchor can't really see the lens very well. The script is printed in large type and very short lines—usually two or three words to the line—so it can be scanned without noticeable eye movement. An operator at the conveyor belt runs the belt to match the anchor's reading speed.

A carbon of the script pages passing by on the conveyor belt is in the anchor's hands. Each time a page goes by, the anchor turns a page on the desk, in case something goes wrong with the TelePrompTer. Sometimes the conveyor belt breaks down, or the operator puts the pages in upside down, or out of order. If that happens, the anchor can continue the story without losing a beat, by glancing down and looking up, a sentence at a time, until the TelePrompTer catches up.

The best anchors glance down at the script on the desk each time they turn a page. They give the illusion that they read the entire page, memorize it, and then recite it to you. If they don't look down occasionally, the viewer begins to wonder why the anchor never looks at the pages being flipped. Maybe they're in braille?

Voice-Over (V/O)

In a voice-over story, the anchor begins to read the story on camera. About 10 seconds into the copy, the director in the control room switches the picture from the anchor to videotape of what the anchor's talking about. The anchor continues to read, live, while you watch videotape. The tape may have sound with it, played very low. This is called *natural sound*. The anchor voice is *over* the picture and any background sound on the tape.

As the anchor talks about last night's Academy Award winner, you see the actor accepting the statuette. If the tape is used with natural sound, you will hear, softly, in the background, the applause when his name is pulled from the envelope.

Voice-Over to Sound (V/O to SOT)

In this version, the anchor begins the story on-camera, just as before. The story becomes V/O as you watch the actor accept the Oscar. Then the anchor stops reading. The sound on the tape is turned up, full volume, and you see and hear the actor thanking his mother, his father, his mistress, his director, and his dog.

For this kind of story, everything must be timed precisely. After the copy is written, a producer with a stopwatch takes it to the anchor, who reads at a normal pace. They time from the point where the live voice-over begins – to where the actor in last night's ceremony will speak on videotape. The voice-over section of tape is edited to run exactly as many seconds as it takes for the anchor to read the copy.

The Countdown

When the anchor reads the copy during the newscast, the director in the control room punches a stopwatch when the voice-over tape begins to roll. The anchor must read for exactly 16 seconds. If the reading is too fast, there will be a hole of silence between the anchor's voice and the actor's. Read too slowly, and the anchor will drown out the beginning of what the actor says. The director works with a microphone and headset. The anchor wears a hidden earphone. The floor crew in the studio all have headsets. By flipping a selector switch, the director can talk to anyone in the studio. As the anchor reads the voice-over section of the story, the director watches the stopwatch and begins a countdown to the floor manager. Ten – nine – eight – seven...

The floor manager hears the countdown on his headset. He holds up fingers, dropping a finger as each second ticks by. The anchor

The director has the entire newscast timed to a split second. As an anchor reads, voice-over, the director calls out the countdown to the floor crew.

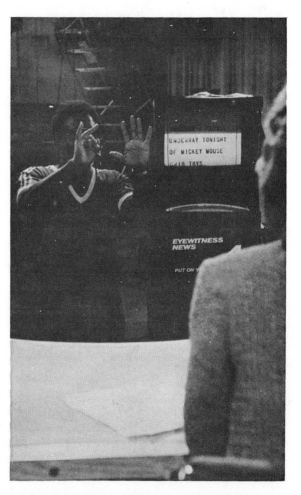

The floor manager hears the countdown on his headset and relays seconds remaining before sound-on-tape. The anchor must finish reading just as the last finger drops.

can see the finger countdown beside the TelePrompTer. When the countdown reaches five seconds, the anchor will hurry a little, or slow down, to finish the voice-over script a split second before the sound-on-tape (SOT) begins. When the Oscar winner finishes thanking everybody, the anchor comes back on camera to begin another story.

11

V/O - SOT - V/O

This is a variation of the same formula. The anchor begins with a copy story, on camera. This is a typical script:

ANCHOR LIVE	THE CITY'S GARBAGE COLLECTORS SAY THEY'LL STRIKE AT MIDNIGHT UNLESS THE CITY COUNCIL GOES ALONG WITH THEIR DEMAND FOR A FIFTEEN PERCENT PAY INCREASE.
V/O (Videotape of meeting)	THE GARBAGE COLLECTORS' UNION MET AT TWO A.M. THIS MORNING, AND WOUND UP WITH A UNANIMOUS VOTE, SETTING TONIGHT'S DEADLINE FOR THE WALKOUT.
SOT (Union president)	"The council says we don't care about our city. Well, I say they don't care about us. We're human beings. Our children have to eat, too."
V/O (Mayor entering City Hall)	THE MAYOR HAS CALLED AN EMERGENCY MEETING OF THE CITY COUNCIL TONIGHT IN A LAST-DITCH EFFORT TO STOP THE STRIKE.

If the story is more complicated – getting the mayor's point of view, for instance – it will usually be handled by a reporter, who will "package" the story.

The Sony Sandwich

The most common formula for a TV news story that involves a reporter is the Sony Sandwich. Some stations call it a "wrap" or a "package." At least half of all television reporters' stories will follow this simple formula. Almost all of them use some variation of the formula. You'll see how it gets its name.

On the air, the story is introduced by the anchor. The anchor copy is called the lead-in. It is a headline, designed to tell you generally what the story is about, grab your attention, and make you want to listen to what the reporter is about to say.

The reporter's entire story is on videotape, both sound and picture. That is why, once edited, it is very difficult to change the length. In the Sony Sandwich formula, the reporter begins by giving viewers the basic facts while she shows what she's talking about. In this case, the natural sound will include sirens and the crackle of the fire under her voice. This is what the script will look like. The notations at the left side of the script are like stage instructions for the director, if the story is read live – for an editor if it will be recorded on videotape.

ANCHOR LEAD-IN
LIVE

FIVE PEOPLE ARE DEAD, THREE

OTHERS MISSING AS THE

RESULT OF A FIRE THAT SWEPT

THROUGH THE UPPER FLOORS

OF A DOWNTOWN ROOMING

13

HOUSE LATE THIS AFTERNOON.
REPORTER DEBBIE DARLING
SAYS FIREMEN SUSPECT ARSON.

Videotape begins.

DARLING V/O
NAT. SO.
(Videotape of
flames)

THE FLAMES RACED SO QUICKLY
THROUGH THE THIRD FLOOR
OF THE OLD WOODEN BARCLAY
HOUSE, FIREMEN SAY
EVERYONE ON THAT FLOOR

(Man jumping)

DIED. ABOVE, FROM A FOURTH-
FLOOR WINDOW, A TERRIFIED
MAN JUMPED TO HIS DEATH
BEFORE FIREMEN COULD RAISE

(Firemen carry-
ing people out)

THEIR LADDERS. THERE WERE
DRAMATIC RESCUES THAT KEPT
THE DEATH TOLL FROM
CLIMBING EVEN HIGHER.

*Now the meat
of the sandwich*

SOT
(Old woman
wrapped
in blanket)

"The smoke was so thick I couldn't
see anything. I knew I was dead.
Then this fireman knocks the
door down, and he throws me
over his shoulder, and goes running right through the flames.
He saved my life."

DARLING V/O
NAT. SO.
(Covered bodies)

(More fire)

(Darling with fire
chief)

THE NAMES OF THE DEAD HAVE
NOT BEEN RELEASED. FIRE
INSPECTORS SAY THE SPEED AT
WHICH THE FLAMES SPREAD
MAKES THEM BELIEVE IT WAS
SET BY AN ARSONIST. WE'LL
HAVE A FULL REPORT TONIGHT
AT ELEVEN. I'M DEBBIE DAR-
LING, EYEWITNESS NEWS.

Chapter 2

How Does It Feel?

The meat in the Sony Sandwich is the interview in the middle. It gives the story flavor and substance. It is sandwiched between the facts the reporter gives at the beginning, and the conclusion the reporter draws at the end. It is so formularized that somewhere in virtually every television news interview, the reporter will ask, "How does it feel?"

How does it feel when you know you have terminal cancer?

How does it feel to win the Nobel Prize?

What were you feeling when you stepped onto the lunar surface?

Reporters are so aware of their trite question, they try to disguise it. But it is still the same search for that magic 10 seconds that will give the story warmth and emotion—the human perspective.

Tell me what you were thinking when the bomb went off.

Are you proud of your son?

Are you angry? Frustrated? Sad? Weary?

How does it feel to do what you did...see what you saw...hear what you heard?

What Was It Like?

More than anything else the reporter can tell us, we want to know what it was like to be there. That has always been the essence of story-telling. If a ghost story is told skillfully, we shudder and look over our shoulder in the dark. Tell me the story of a blind child who can see for the first time, and I get a lump in my throat. When she tells me what she's feeling, I may cry.

Few people outside television understand this basic purpose for the interview.

The reporter does not want many facts

or figures when you are on camera.

There is not enough time to let you tell the facts extemporaneously. Even experienced reporters can't do that. To boil the story down to 20 or 30 seconds may require a half-hour at the typewriter, eliminating a word, rewriting a phrase to save three or four seconds. H.L. Mencken once wrote, "I'm writing you a long letter because I didn't have time to write a short one."

The Story Comes Alive

In that first section of the Sony Sandwich, the reporter quickly sketches the scenario. It is like a line drawing, stark and two-dimensional. The interview fills in the color. The drawing comes alive.

The reporter may edit a series of interviews together – different people giving their reactions to, or perspectives on, the same incident. Or the interviews may pit one point of view against another. A tenant says the landlord refuses to fix the plumbing. Without a pause, the landlord angrily says he's spent $5,000 in the last month on repairs, but the kids in the building tear it up faster than he can fix it.

When sound "bites" are edited against each other, the conflict is distilled quickly and effectively. Instead of watching a ten-round boxing match – mostly dancing, feinting and clinches – we get to see just the knockdowns.

Occasionally, if the sound bite is very strong, it will be placed at the beginning of the reporter's story. In this position, it is normally very short. Then a longer portion of the interview, expanding that opening bite, goes in the middle of the story.

People in certain professions are interviewed more often than others. The ones who get the hang of it find reporters coming back to them on future stories. They make the reporter's job so much easier. Unfortunately, the experience and training for some careers tend to make some people poor interviewees. Most corporate lawyers are terrible on camera. They are accustomed to dry, lengthy, step-by-step reasoning, with lots of footnotes. The simplest question takes them three minutes to answer. This kind of conversation is a horror to edit, as you'll see later. They call the next day and complain that they were quoted out of context.

Human Synthesizers

On-camera police and military officers often become voice synthesizers spouting official reports. The cop who just caught two armed robbers after a shoot-out seems perfectly normal until the camera comes on. Then he says something like:

"This unit was dispatched to 4481 Ocean Street at 8:22 p.m. As I approached, Code Three, I observed two black males rapidly exiting the dispatched location in an easterly direction with weapons drawn. When the subjects observed my vehicle, they commenced firing. I returned the fire. One perpetrator dropped his weapon and surrendered. The other perpetrator continued easterly, then northerly on Front Street, where a backup unit apprehended him and recovered the proceeds of the robbery."

Unusable.

What Do You Think He Said?

What did he say? I think he said:

"As I rolled up, these two guys were running out of the jewelry store with guns in their hands. They saw the patrol car and started shooting. When the first bullet hit the windshield, I jumped out and shot back. One guy dropped his gun and put his hands up. The other ran around the corner, right into my backup. He had his pockets crammed with diamonds and watches."

Which leads to the reporter's question:

"You ever been shot at before?"

"Nope."

"How did it feel?"

"Scared the hell out of me."

Guess which section of the interview is certain to be included in the Sony Sandwich.

People in front of a camera often talk non-conversation because they're afraid they'll make a mistake, or look stupid. They're not sure the boss will like the idea of their talking to a TV camera. They draw themselves into tight little knots, make their voices small and flat, and say every word very carefully. They pause a lot. On television, they are deadly. More than five seconds, and everybody in the audience will be snoring.

Analysis

Emotion and reaction are by far the most common goals of the TV interview, followed by expert analysis. The expert must be able to translate into understandable English. Educators, physicians and engineers are typical professionals who speak strange languages.

After the reporter has said there seems to be no danger from the accident within the nuclear power plant, a recognized expert says on camera:

"We've put the effluent through exhaustive electron microscopy plus radiofluorocarbon laser analysis and we come up with a count of point four, seven, zero micro mini roentgens."

Use an Analogy

Or he can say:

"You'd get more radiation sitting in front of a television set for two hours than you would if you took a bath in the water that leaked out."

Interviews add flavor and spice to a story. Once the conflict, the catastrophe, the crisis are established, we want to hear the participants.

● "The mayor has made a terrible mistake, and I'm going to rub his nose in it." Or:

● "You may laugh at me now, but when I get through, every animal in this entire country will be wearing clothes to hide his nudity. You'll see." Or:

● "I tell you, this guy is completely bonkers."

What's the Story?

Once you understand what the reporter is after, you save a lot of time and anxiety. If you have the chance, talk to the reporter before the camera is turned on. That's the time for names and addresses and details. It will lead to better questions. We'll deal with ambush interviews later.

Some of the best on-camera interviews are with trial lawyers who have spent their entire careers summing up complicated cases for jurors. They keep it short, and simple, conversational and colorful. They're good at one-sentence conclusions jurors will remember and repeat to each other in the jury room. For the main point, they let their feelings show.

Jurors are much like those people sitting in front of the television set after a hard day's work. They're easily bored. They want it simple. They want it interesting. They want to know what it was really like. How did it feel?

One-Liners Guaranteed To Air:

● "Just before we hit the water, all I could think about was my son – that I'd never be able to play ball with him again."

● "Oh, my God, I can't stand this any longer. I've got to get out of here before I go crazy."

● "It's like I'm a kid again. You know, like I've got a whole new life ahead of me."

● "If you had seen as many of my people die as I have, you would understand how much I hate."

● "I didn't have time to be scared. I was too busy trying to get my parachute open."

● "I've been a homicide cop for 15 years, and I've never seen so much blood before."

A Word of Caution:

There are a few rare times when showing your emotions on camera can be hazardous to your career. We don't expect a homicide detective to break down at a murder scene. Unless the victim is his partner, or his own child.

Edmund Muskie may have lost his campaign for the Democratic presidential nomination in 1972 when he cried as he talked about a newspaper editorial that had defamed his wife. That might be acceptable for some professions, but we expect presidents to be tougher than that. We expect leaders to be patient with the people they lead. If you lose your temper on camera – particularly with an employee, or a young reporter – the audience may not forgive you.

What Does It All Mean?

The closing section of the Sony Sandwich is also formularized. The reporter sums up the story. Perhaps tells us what to expect.

"What does it all mean? Only time will tell. I'm Tom Trite, Channel Four, Action News."

Chapter 3

Talking to the Camera

Listening to one end of a telephone conversation, you can often tell who's on the other end. If it's long distance, most people tend to talk louder. Subconsciously, they think they have to speak up to be heard clearly a thousand miles away.

We slow down if the person at the other end of the line has a thick accent. We change the tone of our voice if we're talking to a child, or a lover.

The same kind of subtle changes take place when people talk to television.

On camera, many people subconsciously talk as if they're making a speech at a civic club. There may be half a million people out there listening – but they're not all together, in one place.

The television audience is one or two people, sitting in their living room, about six or seven feet away. One of the secrets of Conversational Television is to keep *that* audience in mind. Television is a very intimate medium. The zoom lens on a camera invades your zone of privacy, moving even closer than a person would, to focus on a drop of sweat, the flared nostrils, the gritted teeth. Or the warmth of a smile.

Think of the Living Room

Part of your preparation for a TV interview ought to be changing your mind-set so you're talking to that small, intimate audience in a familiar living room. It may help you to think of a real living room, and real people. Think of the camera as a specific person, and that may help. The postman, a neighbor, the cashier at the restaurant where you have lunch, the bartender who knows you well enough that you no longer have to order.

Remember, the camera is not one of your professional colleagues. It's somebody you just met at a dinner party, who knows absolutely nothing about your job and won't understand its jargon.

You're not making a speech, or a statement. You're having a conversation.

The Camera Spots Phonies

The camera detects phonies. Bring to that conversation the real person inside you, not a front. Let your emotions show, if they're real. You can be angry, or sad, pleased with yourself or your company, shocked or dismayed at what you've just been told.

Changing your mind-set will change your body language. A politician holds up his arms and flashes a big grin to communicate warmth in the noise and confusion of a political rally. He uses a very different kind of smile and body language if he's trying to charm a beautiful woman sitting across the table in a quiet restaurant.

So, if you know in advance that you'll be interviewed for television, create in your mind the living room, the intimate atmosphere, and the people you'll be talking to.

The FACE Formula

Feelings.

Analysis.

Compelling C's.

Energy.

The FACE Formula will help you remember what the reporter is looking for when you're interviewed for television news. If the audience is going to see your face in the story, keep these factors in mind:

F — **Feelings.** Let the audience know what you're feeling.

A — **Analysis.** Give them your assessment of the situation. In one phrase or sentence, tell them what the bottom line is. The audience wants your opinion on the subject. That's why the reporter is talking to you.

C — **The Compelling C's** of television news. Most television news stories revolve around at least one of these basic elements:

- Catastrophe – "We are facing a national disaster if we don't change the way we dispose of toxic waste."

- Crisis – "That storm is approaching so rapidly, the tidal surge will sweep across the highway and kill a lot of people trying to escape if we don't start the evacuation immediately."

- Conflict – "I feel so strongly about this, I'll fight him to my last breath."

- Crime and Corruption – "Three children are dead, and someone out there is responsible. I intend to find out who did this, and bring him to justice."

- Color – (We used to call it human interest.) "Anyone who believes that also believes that thunder curdles milk."

  More about the Six C's later.

E — **Energy.** There is one major difference in talking for television and talking to your friends in their living room. To be effective on camera, your conversation must project energy. Like a salesman who must believe in his product, you must project that you truly believe what you're saying. Since so many stories for television news involve conflict and imminent danger, you must convince us, through the energy you invest in what you're saying, that we ought to be concerned, too.

Some executives in high-pressure jobs adopt a cool, clinical personality that says to their employees, "I know exactly what I'm doing. If the building were on fire, I could lead you to safety." That deliberate, slow, calculating style can appear, on camera, to be boredom and disinterest.

Forget About Memorizing

Don't memorize, or write what you intend to say when the camera is rolling. It makes the interview look staged and rehearsed. Sections of statements read at live presidential press conferences are about the only prepared statements that make the air.

The first thought that comes to your mind is usually the best and the brightest, and the most sincere. If you start thinking about what you're going to say, it'll be second or third-hand by the time you say it for the camera.

Remember — unless it's a 30-minute talk show in the studio, you have to *condense, condense, condense.* In public speaking courses, the instructor gives you a subject and forces you to make an immediate, extemporaneous talk. The exercise teaches you to think and talk on your feet.

Some TV Training Exercises

Training yourself for television, try to say everything you feel or know about a difficult subject in one sentence. Then pad it out to make 20 or 30 seconds.

Pick tough, complicated subjects and practice with a tape recorder. In one sentence, say how you feel about:

- Abortion
- Nuclear war
- School busing
- Capital punishment
- Prayer in schools
- Suicide
- Communism
- Income taxes
- Welfare
- The Vietnam War

Repeat: Use this exercise only to develop mental agility for condensing what you know and feel about complicated subjects. If you do it while the TV crew is on the way to your office, you'll sound rehearsed and phony.

We'll deal later with antagonistic interviews. For now, let's assume the reporter is friendly, or at least objective – neither warm nor cold.

Do It Early

If you make an appointment for a sit-down interview, try to do it at least four hours before the newscast. The closer to air time, the more harried the crew. They'll do a better job of lighting, shooting, interviewing and editing if they're not pressed against their deadline.

On Your Turf

Choose a place that's comfortable for you. If possible, one that fits the story. If you're a doctor, and you'll be talking about a new surgical technique, do the interview with a backdrop that says *medicine.* If you're a computer programmer, let us see a VDT behind you. It's a real advantage if viewers who turn on their sets in the middle of the interview know at a glance that this story has something to do with doctors or computers.

If you're more comfortable standing while you talk, suggest that to the TV crew.

What's It All About?

It helps if you know generally what the story is about. You can ask when the reporter calls to set up the interview, or during your conversation while the photographer is setting up the lights and camera.

It is considered unethical for a reporter to tell you exactly what the questions will be. The interview is supposed to be a spontaneous conversation. To rehearse either questions or answers is staging. But there is a fine line here. Most reporters consider it proper to tell you the subject they're covering and broad areas they want to explore in the interview.

Don't Cram

For the interview, you don't need to do any cramming. If you, the expert, can't remember, how do you expect viewers to retain what you say? The reporter doesn't want statistics on camera. Go over the numbers before, or after, the interview. Most people can't absorb spoken statistics. They *do* remember analogies. "The money we spend treating this disease would buy everybody in the state a new Cadillac this year."

If the audience is to retain numbers, the story will have to be told with graphs and charts that put them in perspective. Seeing the numbers on the screen helps most people remember them.

The Pecking Order

You should know there is a rigid pecking order within a TV news crew. In most places, the photographer works under the direction of the reporter, and the sound technician is considered the photographer's assistant.

If the reporter doesn't introduce the crew to you, introduce yourself. Remember, the photographer is the one with the power to make the shot flattering, or downright ugly. It never hurts to be on good terms.

Help... Don't Push

You can suggest a place for the interview, but leave the final decision up to the crew. There may be some technical problem with the background of the spot you've chosen. It will take about 15 minutes to set up the equipment. If you're on a tight schedule, let the crew set up while you do something else.

It will help if you know where the electrical panel is, in case their lights overload a circuit.

If the crew is using a small "peanut" mike that clips to your clothing, try to hide the cord. If the mike is clipped to your tie or collar, run the wire inside your shirt to the waist, then inside your waistband to one side.

There's always a clumsy moment when a male sound technician tries to clip the mike to a woman's silk blouse. Help him, so he doesn't feel like he's invading your privacy; and so the alligator clip on the mike doesn't damage your clothes.

Forget the Mike

If they're using a hand-held mike, the tendency is to lean down, or toward the mike. You don't have to do that. It makes you look stoop-shouldered. Forget about the mike. Picking up good sound is their job. If you're not speaking loudly enough, they'll move the mike, or tell you to speak louder.

Talk to the Reporter

During the interview, talk to the reporter, not the camera. The camera is there, listening to the conversation, but it doesn't ask questions. If you answer into the camera, the audience reacts. The reporter asked the question — why are you giving *me* the answer?

The Chair

Swivel chairs are a real hazard. You want to rock in them. The viewer gets seasick as you bob up and down on the tube. Avoid couches and overstuffed chairs where you sink so deeply your arms on the arms of the chair are at shoulder level. Looks like you're hanging from parallel bars.

There's No Hurry

Take your time. If you start a sentence that gets tangled and confusing, start again. That's what editing is for.

If you don't understand the question, say so.

If you're nervous and your mouth is dry, stop for a drink of water. Keep thinking of the living room and the friend or neighbor you're talking to. That will relieve the nervousness. If the lights heat up the room and you begin to sweat, take time to wipe your face.

Short and Simple

Try to talk in short, simple sentences. Lawyers and judges have a tendency to speak in outlined, organized form — firstly, secondly, thirdly — or to label their points A, B and C. Suppose the reporter is only interested in your third point, and you've run the words together, so they can't edit out "thirdly." They may have to throw away the entire section.

Another common phrase: "As I said earlier." There's not enough time in a news story to let you say it twice. If you drop the "as I said earlier" in the middle of a sentence, the entire sentence will have to be dumped.

Any kind of parenthetical thought makes a sentence too long for television.

Example: "I've come to believe, *as most of my constituents do, who've had any experience with firearms,* that every person in this country has the God-given right to own a gun."

It will edit better if the senator says, "I believe every person in this country has the God-given right to own a gun. I'm sure most of my constituents who've had any experience with firearms feel the same way." With this version, the reporter can use either sentence, or both.

Anticipate a Why

Another technique that can help the editing process:

QUESTION: Then you will not vote, Senator, to outlaw Saturday Night Specials?

ANSWER: No.

QUESTION: Why?

ANSWER: The Saturday Night Special is a phony issue.

QUESTION: Why do you say that?

ANSWER: Most policemen, and most store clerks are killed with expensive weapons. Why should the poor homeowner be denied a weapon he can afford to protect himself and his family?

If you give a "Yes" or "No" answer, it will almost always be followed by "Why?" Anticipate the Why. And if you repeat the question as part of your answer, it saves valuable response time between questions and answers. This answer will enable the reporter to cram the entire response into about two-thirds as much time:

QUESTION: Then you will not vote, Senator, to outlaw Saturday Night Specials?

ANSWER: I will never vote to outlaw Saturday Night Specials. They're a phony issue. Most policemen...etc.

Incorporating the question into your answer allows the reporter to drop the sound bite into the story without having to set up what you were asked.

It May Not Be Today

Try not to date what you're saying, particularly if the interview will not be used today. If you talk about something that happened "today" it won't be accurate if the story runs next week.

What You Show Me Speaks So Loudly...

What the audience *sees,* if you're genuine, may communicate more than what they *hear.*

Years ago, advertising agencies learned how to use visual signals in print. A lot can be said in a picture that doesn't require words. Because of television's time limitations, that technique has almost become a science.

Soft drink commercials aimed at teenagers use crowds of tanned, beautiful bodies having fun at the beach. One glance tells the target audience, "Kids who are good-looking, athletic, bright, popular — kids who have enough money to play in the surf with their boats or dune buggies — drink Sexy Cola." All that in half a second, without speaking a single word.

Visual Shorthand

Politicians are learning to use visual symbolism that will carry over from their advertising to television news stories. When he ran for the U.S. Senate, Lawton Chiles campaigned by walking the entire length of Florida. He wore jeans, a work shirt, and heavy walking shoes. All along the way, he stopped to visit and talk with people. Television crews followed him, or met him on the edge of each new town. Little old ladies would come from their farmhouses to give him a glass of water beside the road. At night, there were media pictures of the blisters on his feet.

It Does Take Skill

This kind of technique can be gimmicky unless you have the skill to carry it off. Chiles did. Once his walking campaign was launched, in every television story, no matter what Chiles said, there was another visual message that said, "I'm an ordinary guy, who wants to talk to people, first-hand, about what's bothering them, so I can take their message to Washington. The powerful special interests haven't given me the money to lease a jet, like my opponent. But I'm young, and strong, and I want to be senator bad enough that I'll walk a thousand miles, if that's what it takes, to reach the folks I represent." He managed to say all that, visually, each time he gave a ten-second answer on taxes or solutions to the crime problem.

Clothes

The clothes you wear are part of the visual shorthand. Jimmy Carter liked to be interviewed in a plaid shirt and sweater. His wife wore a plain cloth coat for the inauguration. To enhance his "just plain folks" image, Carter always tried to carry a piece of luggage when he was embarking from a plane or helicopter, even though a small army of aides and Secret Service agents were empty-handed.

Richard Nixon wanted to suggest a more regal kind of presidency. You sometimes wondered if he slept in a coat and tie.

In the early days of television news, men were told to wear blue shirts. That's because they were shooting black-and-white film. A white shirt glowed in the harsh light and high-contrast film. A blue shirt *looked* white when the film was broadcast. With color cameras, white looks white, and blue looks blue.

Generally, your clothes for television should be subdued. Stay away from stripes and checks and bold prints. Don't overdress. A three-piece suit for an interview in your living room may seem as out-of-place as a tuxedo in a cafeteria line.

Hair   If you know the camera is coming, don't go to the beauty salon or the barber shop. This is a spontaneous, unrehearsed conversation, not a portrait gallery.

Jewelry   The goal: Don't let anything about your appearance distract from what you're saying. Large, flashy jewelry is OUT!

Glasses   If you normally wear glasses, wear them for the interview. Without them, your eyes will have to work harder, and you may look very strange.

Sunsquint   If you're being interviewed in bright sunlight, it is almost impossible not to squint. Try this:

Just before the camera starts rolling, close your eyes and look up at the sun. The bright light, coming through your closed eyelids, will contract your pupils. When the camera is rolling, bring your head back down and open your eyes. The pupils will stay contracted for a short time, and you won't sense the glare as much. If you have to talk very long, though, you'll start squinting again.

Suntans

A suntan makes you look healthier and younger. A sunburn makes your skin shiny and puffy.

In-Studio Makeup

For field interviews, women should wear the same makeup they'd wear to work. Lip gloss is too flashy and distracts. If the interview is in a TV studio, the light will be much brighter and harsher. You'll need heavier makeup. Eye shadow and cheek blush should be a tone darker than usual.

Outside the studio, men don't normally use makeup. In the studio, to look normal, you need to wipe pancake makeup across your beard area and the shiny places. The floor crew will have makeup and a communal sponge. You may want to bring your own. It's available in most drug stores, in different shades to match skin tone. To apply, wet a small sponge, rub it on the hard cake of makeup, and then wipe it on your face.

It doesn't smell, and will wash off easily when the interview is over. Receding hairlines and noses are particularly shiny in bright studio lights. And even if they shave just before they go to the TV station, some men with very dark beards look like they just came off skid row.

The idea is to apply just enough makeup to look normal through a studio camera. If it's done right, you can walk out of the studio and nobody will know you're wearing it.

In the Studio

When you walk into the studio, it will seem like a big, cold cavern. The ceiling will be a jumble of black, oddly-shaped stalactites, wires and booms, catwalks and stage lights. Over in one corner, there will be a cozy little set — perhaps a cardboard bookcase or fireplace, or some potted palms — and two chairs, where you and the moderator will do the interview.

Or, it may be a panel show, where you sit facing a group of reporters who fire questions at you. There may be other guests there to debate your point of view.

It's Cold in There

The air conditioning is set low in television studios to counteract the heat of the lights. When they're all turned on, they raise the temperature in the entire studio. If it weren't that cold before the show, you'd probably sweat and be uncomfortable before the show ended. Still, the thermostat is usually set for men who wear coats and ties. Women wearing thin, short-sleeved dresses sometimes turn blue and have to fight to keep from shivering. Long sleeves will help you cope with the cold.

Arrive Early

It's a good idea to arrive about a half hour before the show is scheduled. Producers have nightmares about guests arriving late, or missing the show entirely. It gives you time to get acquainted with the moderator and the other guests. Time to apply makeup. You'll have a better idea of the ground they intend to cover, and you can get used to the strange surroundings.

In some ways, in-studio interviews are very different from field interviews. Most of these shows will not be edited. They're broadcast live, or videotaped for later broadcast just as they were shot. So you have more control over subject matter. Through your answers, you can lead the discussion from one area to another. Your answers can be a little longer. But if you begin to ramble, a good moderator will cut you off, try to force you to answer the question, or move on to the next subject before you've made your point.

Develop... Don't Envelop

When the moderator asks a question, the best standard answer is usually a concise, one-sentence statement of your feeling or opinion, followed by your explanation of why. If you begin to talk too long, and get cut off, you'll still have made your point.

Interview shows work best when there is quick, snappy dialogue between guest and moderator. The quicker the exchanges, the more interesting the conversation seems.

Take Along Your Pictures

If you have videotape, film, still pictures or slides that will help tell your story, let the producer of the show know several days in advance. The producer needs to look at them and decide whether to use them. Then, they'll be ready to put on screen in the control room when you call for them during the show. If you're there to talk about a product, bring it along so the studio cameras can show it while you're discussing it. If you're dealing with a very technical subject, or one that involves a lot of numbers, the producer may want to sit down with you well in advance so the station's artists can sketch or diagram what you're talking about to make it more understandable to the viewing audience.

Avoid the Monitor

In the studio, there will be TV monitors that show what the audience is seeing. After the show begins, avoid the enormous temptation to watch the monitors. It's very difficult not to sneak a look at how you look on TV, but the camera may catch you. Very amateurish.

Pace Yourself

Once the show begins, you need to pace yourself, and be aware of time. If the conversation is lively, thirty minutes goes very quickly, and you may discover that you never got to the main point you wanted to make. If it begins to look like the moderator is not going to reach that area, look for some way to take the conversation there yourself.

"You know, we've danced around this entire subject without getting to what I believe should be our main concern." Then tell us what it is.

Time Signals

There are some strategies that can be played with time segments of the broadcast, particularly if you are debating with another guest. A 30-minute show usually has two or three commercial breaks. The floor crew holds up signs that tell the moderator when to break for a commercial. A big "2" means two minutes. A "30," thirty seconds before the break.

The signal that tells the moderator to hurry is both hands rolling — the same signal a football referee uses to restart the clock. In television, that means speed it up. If they want him to slow down and fill time, the floor manager gives a signal that looks like stretching taffy — "Stretch it out." Waving at the moderator means, "End the show. Tell everybody goodbye." And a finger drawn across the throat means, "Cut it NOW. RIGHT NOW."

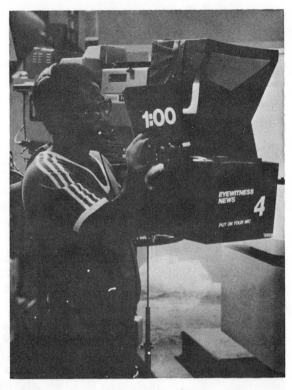

The floor manager signals there is one minute before a commercial break.

If you're aware of those signals, it helps you form an answer that will fit before a break. The moderator won't have to interrupt you in mid-thought.

Time Strategy   If you want to drop your big bomb so the camera can catch your opponent's surprise and fluster, make sure there's enough time before a break. You'll lose the effect if you drop the bomb and the moderator says, "We'll be right back to get the other side's response." That will also give your opponent about two minutes to regain his composure and come up with a good alibi.

Or, you may decide that it's to your advantage to dump your most scandalous accusation just before a break, so the audience has a chance to digest it and let it sink in before your opponent can deny it.

Surprise!   There are few surprise witnesses or shocking new evidence in criminal trials these days. Unlike the Perry Mason era, most rules of court procedure now give each side an opportunity before the trial begins to take depositions from every witness who will testify and to examine every shred of evidence.

One of the attractions of live television debates is the chance that we will see one gladiator catch the other by surprise, spear him to the wall and leave him writhing there in mortal agony. There's no better place to drop new documentary evidence than in front of a live television camera.

The scenario can go something like this:

SENATOR BACKWATER: Nobody has a better voting record than mine when it comes to civil rights issues. I have spent my entire life fighting for justice and equality, regardless of race, creed or color.

CHALLENGER UPSTART: *(reaching into his briefcase)* Funny you would say that, Senator. I just happen to have a picture here of you, at age 21, leading a Ku Klux Klan parade down the main street of the little town where you went to college. I'll hold it up so the cameras can see it.

SENATOR BACKWATER: That's a damned lie. Whatever trash you have there is a phony, cheap counterfeit.

CHALLENGER UPSTART: I thought you might say something like that, Senator, so I did some more research and came up with this column which you wrote for the college newspaper. Let me refresh your memory. In it, you say that blacks – I guess I should quote you directly – you say that "niggers" are genetically inferior and should never be allowed to enter the campus because they would not be able to understand abstract thought or civilized behavior. And I have here a sworn affidavit from the editor of that newspaper, in which he certifies that you are the same Phineas Backwater who led Ku Klux Klan rallies and wrote this essay. I'll make all of this material available to the reporters here in the studio just as soon as this debate is over.

ZAP!

No other forum can match the impact of live, juicy exposure on television. But you must be sure the information is absolutely true. If it's not, you'll be accused of dirty tricks. If you hit below the belt, or take cheap shots, you'll come off shady and sleazy. In the end, you'll be damaged more than your opponent.

Try Not To Evade

If you're on the receiving end of a tough question, television makes an evasive answer much more obvious. Pauses are amplified. It's probably best to answer the question as directly as you can, put your position in its best light, and move on. Use the question that points to your weakness as a springboard to reach your strength.

OTTO MAKER: Yes, we fought the recall of that model because there has not been a single critical injury as the result of a failure of that part. Not one. On the other hand, we voluntarily recalled the 1981 model when we realized we had a problem with a bolt in the rear suspension system. Nobody had to force us to spend 80 million dollars for that recall. We did it voluntarily, once we were able to confirm that there was a problem. And while we're talking about accidents, you should point out the difference in fatal accident frequency for domestic cars versus imports.

Take the Tough Ones First

For best overall effect, get the troublesome questions out of the way early. Then you have the rest of the show to counter with a brighter side. Television producers format their news shows that way. Put all the bad news at the beginning of the newscast. Close the show with a light, funny feature story – a "kicker" that leaves the audience smiling or feeling that maybe everything's not so bad after all.

Live Shots

Most local stations now have the ability to beam back to the studio audio and video that can be broadcast live during the newscast. A standard portable videotape camera is plugged into a microwave transmitter system, usually carried in a van. The van has a collapsible antenna that telescopes 50 feet in the air from the roof of the van. The microwave must then be aimed at the station's receiving antenna. Mountains and buildings can block the signal and make it impossible to transmit from some spots. The antenna sending the microwave beam must be on a line of sight with the receiving antenna. Back at the station, the microwave signal is converted to the broadcast frequency and re-broadcast with no time delay.

The reporter doing a live shot wears an earpiece that allows him to hear what is being broadcast. In that way, he can talk back and forth with the anchors at the studio, and their conversation goes out over the air.

Most live shots are either a reporter standup and conversation with the anchor, or a Sony Sandwich with videotape or a live interview between the reporter's introduction of the story and the summary.

Quickly, Quickly!

If you're interviewed during a live shot, the pressure to condense what you say is greater than in any other interview form. Remember, everything you say is broadcast instantly. There's no chance to edit, and very little opportunity to use cutaways and other video techniques that can keep viewers visually interested while you talk. Many TV news producers believe there is absolutely nothing more boring than a "talking head." If that's all they can get with a live interview, it has to be quick.

Chapter 4

Did I Really Say That?

Editing is an art form. Your interview can be edited so skillfully, you can't tell what they took out, or stitched together. You can't see the scar where a good plastic surgeon makes his incision.

Or – when they've finished editing what you said, you may think the editor used a chain saw.

Once you've given an on-camera interview, you are at the mercy of the reporter and his editor. A very small fraction of what you say in the interview will ever make the air. Maybe none of it. You may wind up on the editing room floor. The usual hallway interview will run about five minutes. A sit-down session, 10 to 20 minutes. Out of that, only about 20 to 30 seconds will be used.

Sound Bites

People who work in television for a while change the way they listen to conversation. At a party, even when they're not working, they find themselves involuntarily scanning what you're saying, marking off usable sound bites. It is like panning for gold. Somewhere in that muddy dialogue, there must be a few bright, memorable nuggets.

Let's watch the editing process.

At a city council meeting, Councilman Luther "Red" Light proposes that the city revoke its current prostitution ordinances. He wants to make prostitution legal in a specially-zoned area near the downtown convention center. A local television crew catches up with him in a hallway after the meeting. He is persuaded to come back to his desk in the council chamber for an on-camera interview. This is a transcript:

1	REPORTER: Councilman, you
2	proposed tonight that the city le-
3	galize prostitution. Why?
4	LIGHT: It seems to me that
5	we've wasted enough time and
6	money and law enforcement re-
7	sources chasing them from one
8	street corner to the next. Have
9	you ever tried to figure what it's
10	costing this town to bring a
11	hooker to court, so she can laugh
12	at the law, pay her $50 fine, and
13	get back on the street in time to
14	catch the lunch-hour customers?
15	It's ridiculous. An absolute waste
16	of time and resources. It's time
17	we had policemen chasing mur-
18	derers and rapists and robbers
19	who terrorize and kill and maim,
20	instead of a few women trying
21	to make a living, supplying a
22	service for which there seems to
23	be a great demand.

24   REPORTER: You say a few

25   women. It's hard for a man to

26   walk from City Hall to the police

27   station without being propo-

28   sitioned. Aren't you just—

29   LIGHT: Exactly. The present

30   law doesn't work. The vice squad

31   made 84 arrests for prostitution

32   last month. You know how many

33   of those arrested spent any time

34   in jail? I'll tell you. None. Not a

35   single one. I've done my home-

36   work on this. The vice squad con-

37   sists of eight detectives, a lieuten-

38   ant and a captain. Ten altogether,

39   who draw total salaries of $23,280

40   per month. Add cars, medical in-

41   surance, other fringe benefits,

42   and the price to the taxpayers is

43   roughly $30,000 per month—

44      $360,000 per year. Now, they ar-

45   rested 84 prostitutes last month

46   —alleged prostitutes. Thirty-two

47   of those arrests were thrown out

48   by the prosecutor's office and

49   never got to court. That leaves 52.

50   Twenty-one of those were dis-

51   missed by the judge. That leaves

52   31. Every one of them pleaded

53   guilty and paid a $50 fine. A total

54   of $1,550 for the city coffers.

55   Why, that won't even pay for the

56   gasoline to run the cars for the

57   vice squad, much less their salar-

58   ies, and the salaries of the clerks,

59   the prosecutors, the judges and

60   secretaries and bailiffs. It's not

61   cost-productive. Never has been.

62   And it doesn't stop prostitution.

63   The world's oldest profession is

64   here to stay. I say zone it into an

65   area where we can control it.

66   Properly done, it might even draw

67   more people to the city. Might

68   as well make some money from it

69   instead of wasting half a million

70   dollars a year, trying to enforce

71   stupid, hypocritical laws that

72   don't work.

73   REPORTER: You realize the

74   preachers will organize to fight

75   your proposal?

76   LIGHT: Sure, I do. But every

77   single preacher knows, down

78   deep in his heart, I'm right.

79   They've got their job to do, I've

80   got mine. But hellfire, this is the

81   20th century. Sex isn't going to go

82   away. It's time we quit pretend-

83   ing it will. I know the preachers

84   will come after me. But in their

85   hearts, they know I'm right.

86   REPORTER: The opponents of

87   legalized prostitution say it in-

88   creases violent crime.

89   LIGHT: What do you think ten

90   policemen fighting crime, instead

91   of chasing little girls down the

92   sidewalk, would accomplish?

93	That's a lot of crap. Put those ten
94	officers to work catching robbers,
95	rapists, killers and thieves, and
96	you'll see the crime rate in this
97	town go down, not up.
98	REPORTER: Thank you,
99	Councilman.

Let's see, now, what a little judicious editing can do. This is what the finished script looks like:

Legalize Hookers
Lead-in

ANCHOR LIVE   CITY POLICE SHOULD QUIT
CHASING PROSTITUTES AND
CONCENTRATE ON VIOLENT
CRIME. THAT'S WHAT CITY
COUNCILMAN "RED" LIGHT PRO-
POSED AT TONIGHT'S COUNCIL
MEETING. NEWSWATCH RE-
PORTER SUSAN SCOOP SAYS
THE COUNCILMAN WANTS TO
CREATE A ZONE FOR LEGALIZED
PROSTITUTION NEAR THE DOWN-
TOWN CONVENTION CENTER.

Videotape begins.

SCOOP V/O (Hookers waving at cars)	THIS IS GOODTIME STREET, JUST TWO BLOCKS FROM THE POLICE STATION. IT COSTS THE CITY ABOUT $300,000 A YEAR TO OPERATE THE VICE SQUAD. COUNCILMAN LIGHT SAYS THE EXPENSE IS A WASTE OF TIME AND MONEY.
SOT Light (Line 80)	This is the 20th century. Sex isn't going to go away...
(Line 29)	The present law doesn't work...
(Line 15)	It's ridiculous. An absolute waste of time and resources. It's time we had policemen chasing murderers and rapists and robbers.
V/O (File tape of vice squad raid)	LIGHT SAYS THE VICE SQUAD MADE 84 ARRESTS LAST MONTH. MOST OF THE CASES WERE DISMISSED BEFORE THEY WENT TO TRIAL. THIRTY-ONE PLEADED GUILTY AND PAID $50 FINES. NOBODY WENT TO JAIL.

SOT Light
(Line 55)

(Line 63)

That won't even pay for the gasoline to run the cars for the vice
squad.... The world's oldest
profession is here to stay. I say
zone it into an area where we can
control it.

SOT STANDUP
(Scoop)

LIGHT SAYS THE CITY'S RELI-
GIOUS LEADERS WILL ATTACK
HIM AND HIS PROPOSAL—BUT
IN THEIR HEARTS, THEY KNOW
HE'S RIGHT. I'M SUSAN SCOOP,
ON THE NIGHT BEAT FOR NEWS-
WATCH ELEVEN.

Here's How They Build a Story

Phrases can be shuffled and spliced together, and your ear can't hear the edit. But editing the video requires some finesse. Here's how they do it:

The reporter first reviews the interview tape and decides which sound bites she'll use. The story will be built around the interview. She may have recorded the interview separately on a small audio recorder. She can listen to it in the car, on the way back to the television station, and save valuable time if she's close to deadline.

When the script is written and approved,

the reporter and editor work together in the editing booth. At most stations, the photographer who shoots the tape also edits it. Networks and stations in very large cities are more specialized. Photographers shoot, and editors edit.

The editing console is two large videocassette recorders (VCRs), each with its own TV monitor. There is a microphone and a sound mixer in the booth. The videocassette recorders are wired together so that what is played on the LEFT VCR can be copied by the RIGHT VCR.

The editor puts a blank videocassette in the RIGHT VCR. The story in its final, broadcast form will be assembled on this cassette.

The script begins with reporter voice-over. Susan reads the first section of script into the microphone. Her voice is recorded on the blank cassette in the RIGHT VCR. There is no picture to go with the voice. That comes later. The RIGHT VCR can record sound, or picture, or both at the same time.

The first sound bite from Councilman Light comes next. The editor puts the interview tape, recorded at City Hall, into the LEFT VCR. He rolls to the section Susan has selected. Susan gives him the "in-cue" – the words at the beginning of the sound bite – and the "out-cue."

In- and Out-Cues

In-cue: "This is the…"

Out-cue: "…going to go away."

Leaving a half-second pause after the reporter's voice, the editor copies from LEFT VCR to RIGHT VCR Councilman Light saying, "This is the 20th century. Sex isn't going to go away." Both audio and video are copied at the same time. Then they search for the next phrase in the script and edit it to the first one – "The present law doesn't work." And then a third one – "It's ridiculous. An absolute waste of resources."

Susan records more voice-over onto the tape in the RIGHT VCR, then another section of edited interview, and finally, Susan's video-taped standup in the council chamber closes the story.

Standups

When we see a reporter talking on camera, it is called a standup. Whether she's sitting, walking, riding or standing, it's still a standup.

If we looked at the tape in the RIGHT VCR now, we would see blank screen while Susan talks; Councilman Light talking; blank screen while Susan talks; Councilman Light talking; Susan talking.

Covering Holes in the Video

They will go back now, to "cover" the video holes in the story. As the crew left the council meeting, they took time to shoot some streetwalkers waving at cars near City Hall. They now edit this video under Susan's voice, mixing in some of the natural sound from the street. The same process puts file tape video of a police raid to cover the second section of reporter voice-over.

Now for the sleight-of-hand that will hide the way they edited what Councilman Light said.

Jump Cuts

The edits are clearly visible. Dramatically visible. You can't miss them. They're called jump cuts. At the beginning of the interview, Light was leaning forward, elbows on his desk. Then he lit a cigar. At one point, he shifted back in his swivel chair and put his hands behind his head.

In the first phrase they edited, Light is puffing on his cigar. The next phrase, butted against it, shows his hands, but no cigar. One arm is on the desk. In the third sound bite, he is leaning back with his hands behind his head. As you watch the edited tape, it looks like the councilman suffers from a strange nerve disorder that makes him suddenly jerk from elbows-on-table to hands-behind-head. He also seems to do magic tricks that make cigars disappear.

At the place where the film or tape is edited, the speaker will suddenly jump to another position. This happens at every edit point. In the early days of television news, they decided jump cuts were too distracting. They developed the "cutaway" technique to hide them.

Cutaways   After they finished the interview at City Hall, Susan and her photographer took several minutes to shoot cutaways. The two most often used cutaways are:

1. A wide-angle "two-shot" that shows both the reporter and the subject of the interview. The interviewee is talking, but the camera is too far away for us to tell whether the movement of his lips matches the words we are hearing.

2. The reporter listening, or the reporter making notes. It is sometimes shot from behind, and over the shoulder, of the person being interviewed. Reporters have a bad habit of nodding during cutaways, like those little toy dogs that sit in the rear windows of automobiles.

How Quickly We Forget

The cutaway shot is edited onto the story cassette for only a second or two. It replaces the picture of the councilman, so that your eyes cut away to something else. The sound is not changed. As soon as the jump cut passes, you see Councilman Light again.

In that brief cutaway second or two, you forget that he was smoking a cigar before you looked away. Your mind assumes that in that cutaway moment, he put out his cigar, or leaned back in his chair. If you diagram the finished videocassette as it will play on the air, it will look like page 55.

Print Also Edits

Print journalism interviews are heavily edited, too. Unless the full transcript is printed, a newspaper story takes a phrase here, a phrase there, often out of sequence. But if the words are direct quotes, the ethics of print require three dots (...) to tell readers where the edit points are. That's the difference. People who work in television understand that a cutaway means an edit point, but most viewers don't know that. Many complaints about television news accuracy and distortion are based on the cutaway editing technique.

But Is That Really What He Said?

"The Selling of the Pentagon," a CBS documentary, caused a major furor — eventually a congressional investigation — in the early 1970s. The criticism was based largely on editing of the interviews. "I said those words, but not in that order," the military spokesman argued. "When you string the phrases together in a different order, it changes the meaning of what I said."

AUDIO TRACK	EDITED VIDEOTAPE	VIDEO TRACK
Reporter voice/over mixed with natural sound		Streetwalkers
Councilman Light's voice	---(EDIT)--- ---(EDIT)---	Light Reporter listening Light
Reporter voice/over mixed with natural sound		File tape of police raid
Councilman Light's voice	---(EDIT)---	Light "Two-shot" cutaway Light
Reporter sound-on-tape shot at City Hall		Reporter standing in council chamber

TV Needs an Edit Signal

If television would create some signal to tell viewers where an interview is edited, much of that kind of criticism could be avoided. During the cutaway, for instance, an audio beep could be inserted to tell the audience an edit took place. If the beep were standardized, it could become television's equivalent of the three-dot ellipsis.

In both television and print, an ethical reporter is very careful to make sure the edited version of an interview does not change the meaning or intent of what was said in the original version.

Jump-Cut Commercials

In the 1960s, the hidden camera was a favorite technique for television commercials. A housewife, supposedly unaware of the camera, was asked to compare her laundry before and after it was washed in Brand X. An old man described his headache in great detail and then told about his miraculous relief after taking two of the new pain killers. Those interviews were heavily edited. Somewhere along the line, somebody said they were misleading if the edit points were hidden with cutaways. So commercials began letting the jump cuts show. As a result, we have become much more accustomed to them. Some news organizations, concerned that they will be accused of distortion, now let jump cuts show in a sensitive interview.

Shooting Reverse Questions

Another editing device uses the "reverse question" between answers. When the interview is finished, everyone is told to stay in position. The photographer shoots cutaways. Then he shoots the reporter asking the same questions asked during the interview. The camera is reversed, shooting in the opposite direction, over the shoulder of the interview subject. The reverse-shot question can then be used as a bridge to get from one answer to another.

Instead of a cutaway at the edit point, we see the reporter asking a question. Then we jump to an answer that may be five minutes away from the last answer. The effect is a continuously flowing conversation. While the question is being asked, the viewer forgets about the cigar or how the person answering the questions was sitting when we last saw him.

The danger in this technique is that the question may not be phrased exactly as it was when you answered it the first time. The new question, spliced to the old answer, may be misleading.

Double-Shooting

On a major network documentary—particularly a sensitive, controversial subject—interviews will be "double-shot." The entire interview is recorded by two cameras—one on the interview subject, the other on the reporter. In that way, reporter questions and reactions are recorded exactly the way the interview subject saw and heard them. There can be no reverse question distortion. But few local stations or network field crews are given the resources to double-shoot interviews.

A Stopwatch in Your Head

The real pros of TV interviewing are congressional leaders who have been interviewed several times a day for the last 20 years. They develop stopwatches in their heads. Before the camera rolls, they discuss the story with the reporter. They get some idea of how their quotes will be used, and how long they'll be allowed to speak.

"How much time do you need?" the congressman says, clearing his throat and brushing his hair aside.

"About 20 seconds," the reporter tells him.

"OK. Ready?"

"Rolling."

The congressman speaks for 20 seconds. Perhaps 19. Sometimes, 21. And then he stops. He has learned the language, and the game. He edits himself. There can be no distortion. He is rarely quoted out of context.

Really, You Can Do It, Too

Most of those who've learned to speak television did it the hard way, through trial and error, almost by accident. For many, it became a self-defense tactic. The news media are kinder to some people than others. One man's slip winds up on the cutting room floor. Another, similar bumble becomes the "kicker" on tonight's news.

Watch television news, and make notes on the people who are effective in their interviews. Learn from the mistakes and blunders of other people. If you're in a position where you expect to be interviewed regularly, ask for a guided tour of the local newsroom and editing facilities. If you can, spend a day with a camera crew, watching them shoot, write, and edit a story. The more familiar you become with the entire process, the easier it will be to adapt your speaking style to the medium.

Learning to speak television requires some concentration. But it's a lot easier than Spanish or German.

You can do it.

Chapter 5

Why Do They Always Bring Bad News?

The side dish with most American dinners now is a generous helping of blood and guts. Night after night, we watch bodies dragged across the screen. If not a double murder, then a plane crash. If not a terrorist bombing, then a tenement house fire, with mothers dropping their babies to the pavement. Why does television always bring bad news?

Because people want to see it.

Because they *need* to see it.

It is not just morbid curiosity. It is part of our instinct for self-preservation. We *need* to know there is a killer stalking children so we can protect our children. We *want* to know there is a serious design defect in a new airplane so we can take a different flight. We have always pictured ourselves as caring people who value human life. But because most of us never venture into the ghetto, we do not think about inadequate or unenforced building codes until we see children die.

We have become so isolated from each other, so insulated from our own neighborhoods, we do not notice problems unless there is a disaster to grab our attention. In a nation so overloaded with crises, we seem now to tend only those that have most recently shocked and sickened us.

We Are Insulated from Life

There is another theory, too, about the crowds that gather to stare at people dead, or dying, in the street. In this sterile, high-tech society, most of us never see or experience life's most basic components. Most of us have never seen the struggle and wonder of birth, the anguish of a nervous breakdown, the courage of self-sacrifice, the loneliness of old age.

Most of us have never seen someone die.

We hide life's basics in hospitals and nursing homes, or in a code of behavior that says we must never, never let anyone know what we are feeling, or who we really are.

We are terribly alone, and often bored, in our plastic packages. We need to touch reality. And so we are drawn to – fascinated by – death and violence, human triumph and tragedy. That is one reason cops and reporters and doctors are the central figures in so much of contemporary television drama. Their jobs put them in touch with humanity. We want to look over their shoulders. We envy their opportunity to experience life with the wraps off.

How Much Gore?

In television newsrooms everywhere, there is constant debate over just how much to show. How much blood should they let seep into your living room? How close shall the camera zoom in on the face of the dead child?

There are excesses, and after a long string of bodies every night, news directors write memos ordering less blood and gore. Television news is always trying to sense just the right balance. Enough to satisfy the viewers' cravings – not so much to disgust them and make them switch stations. Enough to inform and motivate without turning them – and their sets – off.

We Forget Good News

There is another phenomenon here. We remember the BAD NEWS stories and forget the rest. In almost every television newscast, there are lots of GOOD NEWS stories. Many local stations now have their equivalent of Charles Kuralt On The Road. Folksy visits with little old ladies who still chop wood for their kitchen stoves. Trained pigs that bring in the newspaper. Kids that have defeated birth defects through sheer courage and determination.

For some reason or another, we forget the story about the cop who saved a life, and remember the story about the one who sold his badge to the dope peddler.

The Mayor Was Sober Today

News is the unusual.

If the anchor says, "The mayor was sober today," we assume he is drunk most of the time. What would your reaction be if tonight's newscast told you:

- No children were murdered today.
- There were no major airline crashes today.
- No bridges collapsed, and no politicians were arrested for bribery today.

News Is What's Different

News is something different.

It is news when a Vietnam veteran threatens to leap from the roof of a downtown building. It is not news that thousands of other veterans went about their daily lives, never thinking of suicide.

We assume that everything is OK. News is the exception. Something that is not OK. When television reports that a government official has been arrested for bribery, we assume that thousands of others were honest.

News Is Information You Need

News can also be more than just the unusual. It can be information people need. Information that will in some way affect their lives. In a democratic society, we need to know that the school board is contemplating a tax increase so we can support or try to stop it. We

61

need to know that a certain brand of sardines is contaminated so we can throw them away and not get seriously ill.

Unfortunately, many of the stories that are staples for newspapers are not visually interesting. Videotape of the school board's hearing on property taxes is not nearly as exciting as a warehouse fire. Because the number of people watching is so critical to television profits, the decision is easy. Air the fire. Dump the hearing. The school board didn't decide anything, anyway.

Compelling C's of TV News

There are six broad categories for television news stories — the six Compelling C's:

Catastrophe

Crisis

Conflict

Crime

Corruption

Color (We used to call it human interest.)

If you, your agency or your company are going to be on television, you will usually have some story angle that fits at least one of these categories. And it must be unusual.

"My civic club elected officers last night, and I thought you might want to do a story," the caller tells the assignment editor. In a television market area, there are hundreds — perhaps thousands — of civic club elections each year. Not news.

Another caller says, "I don't want to give you my name, but you should look into what's happening at the Zebra Club. The treasurer embezzled $200,000 and ran off with the president's wife. The children's hospital we support is about to close its doors. They're running out of money because of the theft. There's a big internal fight now, on whether to prosecute the treasurer, or hush it up. Oh, by the way, the treasurer is a Catholic priest."

Now, That's News

Now, that's news. Crime, corruption, crisis, conflict, color.

Back to the school board budget hearing. LIGHTS. CAMERA. ACTION.

School board member: "Looks to me like the school superintendent has sold out **(corruption?)** to the realtors who are fighting this tax increase **(conflict)**. If this tax is not approved, we may have to shut down some of our schools **(crisis)**."

Veteran politicians understand the technique and use it all the time to get TV news coverage. The people they attack understand it's nothing personal. They go on camera to fight back, and their point of view gets aired. A lot like attorneys who seem to have a grudge match going in court, but play golf together every Sunday.

It Is a Game

It is a game, very much like professional sports. To communicate effectively, you need to learn the game. It must be played very skillfully. If TV reporters suspect they are being manipulated with a phony issue, the technique will backfire.

One reason professional sports are so popular is that they incorporate most of these basic elements. **Conflict** is central — one team using all its resources to beat the other. There is a new **crisis** every week—what happens if they lose? **Catastrophe** when the star quarterback is injured. And **color** everywhere. Rugged, macho players. Sexy cheerleaders. Big money. Crowds, music, applause. The glory of it all.

In news, the game is life and death.

Don't Tell Me – Show Me

In newsrooms all over the world, there is a sign: Don't Tell Me—Show Me.

It is a reminder to reporters and photographers that the story *must* be visual. We are no longer satisfied to read or hear about someone trying to shoot the president. We want to *see* and *hear* the assassin, in living color and natural sound.

Sports coverage, again, illustrates state-of-the-art television. Half a dozen live cameras shooting from every conceivable angle. At least one camera always at the point of impact, much closer than if we had 50-yard-line seats. It can replay the fumble or the winning pass again and again, in slow motion, so we can study and savor it.

Unfortunately, much of government and business is dull, by comparison with other, more visual stories. How do you show a smooth-running water department? How do you photograph a record stock dividend? So much of government that was traditionally covered by newspapers is almost entirely ignored by television. Even Watergate—the biggest story of the 1970s—was poorly covered by television. There was little that television could *show* until the impeachment hearings began. Most of the Watergate story had to be *told.*

Remember: Don't Tell Me—Show Me.

TV Needs Beat Reporters

As more people get their news from television, the democratic process will be diminished, unless television decides to invest in full-time beat reporters who spend their entire day at the courthouse or city hall. Clever, inventive reporters who can find new ways to tell government stories visually. Stories with movement and color, conflict and crisis, and sometimes – corruption.

But if television does a poor job of covering government, it does a superb job of covering presidential campaigns. From the early primaries through the conventions, to national debates, to election night and the inauguration, the networks throw every available resource into their coverage. They invest enormous amounts of time and money and their very best talent, both on and off camera.

Why?

Frantic, coast-to-coast action. Visual excitement and suspense. Conflict. Crisis. Catastrophe. Color. And always lurking there – the possibility of a juicy scandal. Corruption.

Chapter 6

The Battle for Viewers, Ratings and Money

Television is probably America's most fiercely competitive industry. Very slight shifts in the number of people watching your station or network can mean millions of dollars.

It is an industry constantly in metamorphosis, looking for some new game or gimmick that will entice a few more people away from the competition. If the audience wants a little more sex, a little more violence, that's what it gets. Each producer is constantly trying to guess next season's fad or fashion, hoping he can invent a show or character or situation that will play to the appetite of that fleeting, fickle audience.

Once a show becomes a success, there is a stampede to copy and clone it, hoping to squeeze every penny of profit out of the idea before it gets stale and the audience moves on to whatever turns them on. "All in the Family" becomes "Archie Bunker's Place," until the audience eventually becomes weary of the characters and dwindles away. "Happy Days" breeds "Laverne and Shirley."

At the top, television news is controlled by the same people who program entertainment. They are always looking for the magic formula that will seduce people away from the competition. If they suspect the audience wants more flash and trash, then flash and trash becomes the lead story.

From city to city, television news is as varied as radio station formats. There are newscasts anchored by gray-haired veterans as bland and dated as elevator music.

Hard Rock News

In other markets, young, hyper anchors almost shout stories in a style similar to hard-rock radio. It doesn't matter so much what the words say, so long as you keep the rhythm and beat. Keep it frantic.

"The City Manager's Secret Agony! Tape at Eleven!"

"A Psychic Says UFOs Will Disrupt The Governor's Inauguration! I'll Talk With Her Live, at Five!"

How do you know how many people are watching? How do you know they'd rather learn about a new diet than the defense budget?

Ratings

As a general rule, the cost of commercial time on television is based on how many people will see the advertising. Thirty seconds of commercial time in a small town, after midnight, can cost as little as $10. In a major city, a locally-produced special in prime time can charge as much as $15,000 for half a minute.

Thirty-second network commercials in prime evening hours average about $75,000. But a one-minute commercial during a Super Bowl telecast can top a half-million dollars. In early 1983, the last installment of "M*A*S*H" set a new record— $450,000 for each 30-second commercial.

Nationwide, advertisers pay about eight billion dollars for commercial time on TV each year.

How do they know they're getting the audience they pay for?

Nielsen and Arbitron

Two national rating services— A.C. Nielsen and Arbitron— constantly monitor how many people have their sets turned on, and which

67

shows they're tuned to.

The rating services use three different techniques to measure the audience:

- Telephone surveys.
- Viewer diaries.
- Viewing meters.

For all three methods, the rating services develop small, random samples that are supposed to accurately reflect the TV audience. Arbitron's specialty is large telephone surveys. Nielsen developed the technique of locating a representative family and giving them a diary to log what they watch, making an entry every 15 minutes when the set is turned on. Once a family agrees to keep a diary, their viewing habits are monitored for long periods of time. Their identity is a secret, to avoid any outside influence on their choice of shows.

How To Read the Rating Numbers

Programs are measured in two ways:

Rating – the percentage of the population that owns a TV set that watched a program.

Share – The percentage of people watching television at the time who were tuned to a particular program.

If a town has a thousand people in it and 50 are watching television – but all are watching the same show – then that show will have a 5 Rating/100 Share.

A program with a 12 Rating/26 Share was watched by 12 percent of the households *who own TV sets* in that market and by 26 percent of the households who were *watching TV* during its time slot.

Rating numbers go up during prime time at

night, when more people watch television. Share numbers in any market total 100, no matter how many people are watching.

In addition to the rating and share figures, the services report detailed demographic information on the people watching, by age, sex, ethnicity, and whether the woman in the household is employed. They report whether the households have cable or pay TV.

Special Services

If a station wants to know about its audience, it can arrange for the rating service to expand the information on each household in the sample. Questions like whether they own or rent their home, education, occupation, income, and whether they use certain types of products.

All this can be useful to advertisers who want to target a certain audience.

The "Sweeps"

The standard rating periods take place four times a year — in November, February, May and July. You'll notice local newscasts promoting themselves a lot more during the rating "sweeps," trying to improve their numbers so the sales departments can increase the price of advertising. At many stations, special reports and series are broadcast only during rating periods.

Because almost all advertising prices are based on those ratings, *who* watches is sometimes more important than *how many.*

Advertisers are particularly interested in 18- to 49-year-olds. They're the consumers in our society — the ones who earn more, and spend it more freely. A newscast ranked second in terms of total audience can charge more for its advertising time if the ratings show it outdraws the Number One station in 18- to 49-year-old viewers.

Meters

In 1972, Nielsen began using viewing meters in New York City to supplement its telephone surveys and viewer diaries. The company selects a household in the same statistical way it chooses a family for a telephone call or a diary.

The family gives its permission for the rating service to connect a meter to its TV set.

Any time the set is turned on, the meter automatically keeps a record of which station it's tuned to. By 1983, the metering technique had spread to six market areas—New York, Los Angeles, Chicago, San Francisco-Oakland, Philadelphia and Detroit.

Those six markets contain one-fourth of all the television viewers in the United States. The meters are connected by telephone lines to computers, so that instant ratings can be tabulated. They work 24 hours a day, year-round, instead of just during "sweep" periods.

"Voting" a Show

In some ways, meters are much more accurate than telephone and diary reports. Rating services have learned that people in viewing samples have a tendency to cheat. If they have a favorite series, they "vote" for it, reporting that they watched it, even if they didn't.

Viewers also tend to tell the rating service they watched shows they think they should watch. They may say they saw a National Geographic special or a concert when they were really watching the Three Stooges.

Meters eliminate the inaccuracies of diaries in families that have literacy or language problems; or families that get sloppy, and fill out their diaries at the end of the week, relying on memory to report what they watched.

But meters have their own inaccuracies. They report viewers if a set is turned on, even when nobody is watching it. When a family gives permission for a meter to be installed, they seem – for a while – to watch a lot more television than the norm. There's a subtle psychological effect.

Meters Make You Watch More

Their inclusion in the sample makes them feel like their choice of shows has suddenly become more important. That tendency to increase viewing time slacks off after several months. The families aren't told this, but the rating services usually don't start tabulating their viewing until that early period of heavy TV watching has passed.

Independent stations seem to be the big winners when meters replace diaries and telephone surveys. One study, done in November, 1979, shows daytime ratings for independents double after meters are installed. The analysts can only guess why.

The Meter Mystery

Under the old systems, housewives may have been "voting" for certain shows, while they were actually watching old movies or wrestling. Or – they may have used independent stations' re-runs to babysit small children. Another explanation could be that they didn't want their husbands to know how much time they spent watching daytime television, and simply didn't report their viewing accurately in viewing diaries.

Meters seem to make little difference in ratings and shares during prime time, from 8 to

11 p.m. But after 11 o'clock, that same 1979 study shows the ratings of independent stations 42 percent higher. That late-night difference is harder to explain than the daytime discrepancy between diaries and meters.

Why Anchors Are Paid So Much

Slight shifts in audiences mean millions of dollars. If a network show increases its ratings just one point, that means another two and one-half million people watched the broadcast and absorbed its commercial messages.

That's why on-air "talent" — particularly anchors and sportscasters — are paid so much. One of the most striking examples of an audience shift because of one performer took place in New York City in the summer of 1980. For a long time, WCBS had been second in the ratings to WABC during the six o'clock newscasts. In a move to change that, WCBS stole sportscaster Warner Wolf away from WABC, for a reported salary of $400,000. Within two weeks, WCBS's six o'clock newscast was in a dead heat with WABC. And at 11 o'clock, Wolf's switch to WCBS helped his new station pull ahead by two rating points over WABC. The fans Wolf brought with him were clearly worth several times more than his annual salary, through increased advertising revenue for WCBS. Most rating changes are much more gradual.

It's not unusual now for a popular anchor in a major local market to earn a quarter-million-dollar salary, plus all kinds of "perks" — a chauffeured limousine to commute between home and work; an extravagant expense account and clothes allowance, a reporting assignment outside the country at least once a year, where he can bring the wife and kids along.

Network anchors are even more pampered.

"Hi, Dan." Television is an unusual medium. Its anchors have more celebrity status than anyone except the President of the United States. Walk a movie star and Dan Rather down the same sidewalk, and many more people will recognize Rather. More than just recognize him — they'll speak, wave, call him Dan. They think they know him on a personal basis. If you questioned them they'd have a complete personality in mind, all based entirely on their perceptions of him from his visits in their living room every evening.

The ability to create that kind of relationship with viewers is an extremely valuable commodity.

Shooting Craps Because the ratings are so critical and so fluid, television news is in a constant state of flux. If the ratings get stuck or go down, you change the format or the pacing or the people.

It's like shooting craps. If the new anchor or weather forecaster or news director doesn't bring the ratings up, fire him and try another roll of the dice. You keep changing people until you hit a winning combination.

Consulting firms charge small fortunes to study newscasts and newscasters, looking for the magic formula that will increase ratings. They lock test viewers in rooms, show them videotape, and then debrief them on what they saw, what they liked, what they remember.

Consultants The consultant tells the station to fire the sportscaster. He's not macho enough. Get a sexy weatherwoman. Change the anchor's haircut, or clothes. Build a new set that looks like a space station. Have the talent talk to each other more during the newscast. Make it look like they truly enjoy each other's company, and what they're doing.

There are millions of combinations to try, always in pursuit of some subtle effect that will make more people switch to a station — particularly 18- to 49-year olds. Once a prescription works in one city — like the "happy talk" formula in the 1970s — the consultants race from station to station across the country, selling their new cure for ratings sickness.

In Search of the Magic Elixir

And, like magic, it works. For a while. Until some other consultant comes up with another elixir that will lure viewers.

The process never stops.

All this may seem terribly phony and money-grubbing. But it is the way the system works. Capitalism and free enterprise in their purest forms.

Television is not going to disappear. The candidate who chooses to run a whistle-stop campaign from the back of a Pullman car instead of using TV spots will wind up in some obscure train yard, talking to himself.

Communication today is 12-second thoughts, packaged with subliminal hints and human chemistry to create the total message. Some people can do it naturally. For others, it is a skill that must be mastered.

There are purists who balk at the idea; who say television is ephemeral and shallow; that its performers are pretentious and plastic; that its motives are crass and demeaning.

At times, and to some extent, all of those criticisms are valid.

But when TV is good, it is very, very good. No other technique has yet been invented to reach so many people so quickly and with such power.

Networks

The relationship between the networks and their local affiliates is confusing. Many people think of their hometown newscast as "ABC's local news," or "CBS in Atlanta."

The tie between a network and its affiliates is much more distant than that.

Networks and local stations have contracts to supply services to each other. But there's usually no ownership interest between the two.

O and O's

The exceptions are 15 network-owned-and-operated stations. In the business, they're called "O and O's."

The FCC limits the number of television outlets one company can own to five VHF stations (channels 2 through 13) and two UHF stations (channel 14 and higher). The rule was established to prevent monopolies that could narrow the control of television news. Each network owns the maximum five VHF stations.

They are:

ABC
New York — WABC-TV
Chicago — WLS-TV
Los Angeles — KABC-TV
Detroit — WXYZ-TV
San Francisco — KGO-TV

CBS
New York — WCBS-TV
Chicago — WBBM-TV
Los Angeles — KNXT
St. Louis — KMOX-TV
Philadelphia — WCAU-TV

NBC
New York — WNBC-TV
Chicago — WMAQ-TV
Los Angeles — KNBC
Cleveland — WKYC-TV
Washington — WRC-TV

No Network Control

At about 740 other commercially-operated stations around the country, the networks have no ownership interest, and no control over local programming.

(The number of stations varies slightly from year to year as new stations are added. About 520 of the commercial stations are VHF, the rest UHF. There are about 270 educational channels — a little over 100 of them VHF stations. Of the commercial stations, about 150 are independent, and the rest are network-affiliated.)

Money Is Based on a National Audience

The entire network structure and financial base depend on a national audience. When advertisers buy network time, they want to reach the entire country. So the network has a contract with a local station in each market area to broadcast network programming in that area. The local affiliate has some options to pre-empt network programming, but they're severely limited. The network wants to be sure that its advertising will reach the mass audience it promised when it sold the commercial time.

In return for that service, the network pays the local station a fee. The fee is negotiated with each station, and varies according to market size. It's not a large fee. Not much more than it costs to provide the equipment, engineers and overhead to keep the local station on the air for network shows.

The Local Cut

In effect, the local affiliate gets free network programming to fill most of its broadcast day.

The real money for the affiliate comes from local advertising slots that are built into network programming. For each hour of network shows, there will be about two minutes where the station can insert local commercials. The money the affiliate gets for those commercials is pure profit.

Watch a network show. Most of the advertising will be national – cars, detergents, aspirin, beer or office machines. But one of the commercial breaks – perhaps two – will advertise Aunt Millie's Delicatessen or a local diaper service.

The cost of producing an hour of entertainment is more than you could sell the commercial time for in a local market. There just aren't enough people in one city to justify the kind of advertising rates necessary to pay for those shows.

Many local news operations cost more than the advertising they bring in. A documentary that requires travel halfway around the world and six months' work by a reporter and camera crew will cost more than the local commercial time in that hour can earn.

There is usually a cooperative working relationship between network news organizations and the local stations. Suppose a tornado touches down in your area. There's no network correspondent available to cover the story. The network will call the local affiliate and ask for a copy of its tornado videotape.

Locals on the Network

Sometimes, the network will ask for a complete "package" from a reporter at the local affiliate. When the reporter "sigs out" at the close of the story, you can tell whether he's network or local. If he's local, he says, "In Topeka, I'm William Windy, for NBC News." If the story is done *for* the network, the reporter is not part of the network staff. When a network uses videotape shot by an affiliate, it usually pays the reporter and camera crew a fee. They're moonlighting for the network.

If the network news desk decides to send a crew to a town where it has no bureau, the crew will often use the local affiliate's newsroom, telephones and editing facilities. The same cable and satellite systems that bring network programming to the local affiliate can also be used to transmit stories to New York or Washington for tonight's network newscast.

The Rise of News

Until the middle 1970s, news was rarely a money-maker for local stations or networks. It was considered a prestige item, which built viewer loyalty for entertainment shows.

But something happened — perhaps Watergate — to make Americans news-hungry. With the exception of an occasional special program or blockbuster movie, "60 Minutes" became the most-watched television show on the air in the early 1980s.

There are millions of news junkies who will watch three and four hours of news at a sitting, even if many of the stories are repeated, in slightly different form, every 30 minutes. Cable and satellite news services now offer 24-hour, non-stop news. When Ted Turner started his first Cable News Network in 1980, few people believed the country could absorb that kind of news saturation. Most of the experts thought Turner was on an ego binge that would drive him to bankruptcy. Instead, he opened a second non-stop Cable News Network in 1982, with quicker, shorter stories. And in that same year, ABC and the Westinghouse Broadcast Group combined forces to create their own non-stop news service, delivered by satellite.

Independent News Networks

The independent news networks have made local independent stations more competitive. Stations with no network affiliation have to buy their programming from syndicates and independent producers. Until the 1980s, independent stations generally ran very old movies and sit-com re-runs. To meet FCC requirements, they usually had some sort of local newscast. But the size of the staff – and the quality of their work – was usually vastly inferior to their network affiliate competition.

Those independents can now buy slick, independent network newscasts that give international and national coverage and vastly increase the prestige of the independent station. Those independent networks also give cable systems news to compete with both the local affiliates and the networks.

Early Risers Like 10 O'Clock News

Independent stations also have more flexibility in scheduling their programs. In the South and Northeast, for instance, network programming runs until 11 p.m. Most local affiliates run their late-night newscasts at 11. But a lot of people can't stay up that late, so many independents run their newscasts at 10 p.m. A substantial chunk of the audience will switch from network programming at 10 o'clock so they can catch up with the news before they go to bed.

Chapter 7

Boy, Have I Got a Story For You

Television misses many stories simply because it doesn't know about them in time to get a camera there. A big newspaper will usually have about five reporters for each reporter at a TV station.

Newspapers assign reporters to beats, and those reporters spend their entire day at city hall or the courthouse or the police station. They're expected to know, and report, absolutely everything that goes on there.

Television depends largely on viewers who call to tip them to stories.

The assignment editor is the person who decides each morning how his reporters and photographers will be dispatched. If you'd like to have TV coverage of something you're involved in, you need to let the assignment editor know about it. Before you call to tell him about your Saturday night bridge club, though, you should know a little more about his job and what he needs from you.

The Assignment Editor

Assignment editors are probably the most harried people in television news. The typical assignment editor sits in the center of the newsroom, totally immersed in noise and confusion. He has to answer a bank of telephones that are constantly ringing. He must monitor several squawking police and fire department radio scanners, to make sure he doesn't miss a fire or a murder.

At some stations, he also eavesdrops on the two-way radio conversations of the newspaper photographers and the competing television stations to hear what they're covering. On top of that, a dozen of his own photographers out in their cars need directions to addresses they can't find. They are reporting by radio every few minutes to tell him their camera or tape recorder has broken down; that they arrived 30 seconds too late to catch the bridge collapse; that the convention he sent them to doesn't begin until next week, that the massive protest against police brutality is actually a little old man who hand-delivered a letter to the mayor's secretary.

No Respect

If the assignment editor happens to get his crew to the right place at the right time, and they come away with a great visual story, the reporter and photographer usually get the credit. If the assignment editor misses a story, the news director has a nasty habit of screaming and banging his fist on the desk.

Good assignment editors are born. Those that aren't, but try to remake themselves into assignment editors, often have nervous breakdowns.

Is It Really News?

Before you call or write the assignment editor at your favorite television station, go back to Chapter Five and review the elements that make events and people newsworthy.

Does it involve one of the Six C's?
Is it unusual?
Is it visual?

Let the assignment editor know, in writing, several days in advance. Then give him a call late in the afternoon the day before your story is to be covered. By late afternoon, the most hectic part of his day is over. The crews are back in the newsroom, writing and editing their stories for tonight's newscast. The assignment editor is outlining tomorrow's assignments. Ask if he needs anything else that will help him cover your story.

Try not to push, or gush. If it's a good story, he'll know it. It doesn't have to be sold. There may be an element that's not obvious. You need to tell him about it. What makes it so unusual?

Don't Cry Wolf

Public relations firms have a bad habit of trying to sell stories that really aren't newsworthy. Once an assignment editor gets burned by sending a crew to a story that isn't, he's less likely to believe that you've got a good one next time.

Television news is terribly understaffed. Camera crews spend the entire day rushing from one story to another. Give the assignment editor accurate times so his crew won't waste valuable minutes waiting for people to show up or the event to begin.

TV or Newspapers?

If the story is not an event that needs to be photographed, you sometimes have to decide whether to give it to the newspaper or television, or to both at the same time.

In most cities, newspapers tend to ignore television. If television beats them to a story, they won't touch it. If it's good enough, they'll revive it several weeks later, with a new twist, trying to make it look like they found the story and broke it exclusively.

Television is not so concerned about competing with newspapers. News directors will kill to beat a competing TV station to a story, but they figure most viewers don't read newspapers. Just because it's in the newspaper this morning doesn't make it any less news for their audience.

The rivalry between TV and newspapers over being first with a story varies from place to place. You have to test it in your market area.

Some PIO's and public relations agencies give stories to the newspaper, without calling TV. The newspaper coverage makes TV more interested in a story that may be visually dull.

It Happens at the Networks, Too

The same phenomenon takes place with national stories. Network bureaus send story proposals to New York. New York says it's not interested, and the story idea is trashed. Two months later, the story appears in the *New York Times* or *Washington Post.* The network news desk in New York jerks the bureau chief in Los Angeles out of bed at 5 a.m., telling him to get the story for tonight's newscast.

"Hey, I told you about that story two months ago, and you didn't want it," the grumpy bureau chief complains.

"It wasn't news then," New York says.

Public Affairs Programs

Most local stations produce other types of news-related programs that are the responsibility of the public affairs director. Interview shows on weekends; early morning shows that feature invited guests; audience call-in shows, and late-night shows that may have a studio audience are often produced locally. Some of them have regular guests, like the county agent in farm areas, who gets ten minutes every day at 5:30 a.m. The county agent's time slot was apparently chosen because they thought the farmer audience had to be up that early to milk the cows.

Public affairs directors are usually hungry for ideas and guests, particularly if they can be tied in some way to a current news story.

If you're looking for ways to get your message or your people on television, watch for an opportunity in public affairs programming, where you can be an expert on some item in the news. If you turn out to be a good interview subject, the news director and assignment editor will remember, and come to you for comment when they need expert analysis for future news coverage.

Press Releases

For television coverage, the written press release *in news story form* is obsolete. The trash cans of assignment editors across the land are crammed with press releases prepared by high-priced public relations firms whose clients don't understand why the story never made the air. Television considers them another form of junk mail.

The press release was invented to cater to lazy newspaper people. Since it was written in newspaper style, a lazy editor or reporter could simply re-type it, word-for-word, and put it in the paper. In the bad old days, some sleazy reporters would even put their own by-lines on the story. Public relations people loved it. They could not only plant stories, they could actually write them exactly as they wanted them to appear in print. It was better than free lunch in the old-time saloon.

Advance Notice

What television *does* need is advance notice in writing or by phone, so they can have a camera there. Simple, one-paragraph letters will do, addressed to the assignment editor:

"Mike Megawatt will speak to the Chum and Chowder Society next Tuesday at 12:30 p.m. in the Anthracite Hotel. He'll talk about the company's requested rate increase and the Power Company's petition to burn coal in the Smoky Hollow plant. We hope to have copies of the speech available for your reporter shortly before the meeting begins."

Fact Sheets

If you're opening a new plant, send the assignment editor a fact sheet, not a flowery news story. Something like:

Cost — $18.6 million.

Building Contractor — Saw and Hammer Corp.

Construction time — 21 months.

Square feet — 92,500, all air-conditioned.

Special features — Employees' cafeteria, swimming pool, gymnasium, solar panels to heat water and generate electricity.

Number of employees to work here — 2,150.

Expected production capacity — 6.6 million widgets per year; retail value, $134 million, to be sold east of the Mississippi and in Central and Latin America.

The assignment editor will give the fact sheet to the reporter covering the story. It will help him ask better questions, and give him some idea of what he wants to photograph before he arrives at the plant opening ceremony.

Obsolete Forms

Press releases churned out by federal law enforcement agencies often follow the rigid form J. Edgar Hoover perfected in the 1940s. Every press release began: "FBI Director J. Edgar Hoover announced in Washington today..."

The form changed during a brief time in the early 1960s when Robert Kennedy was U.S. attorney general and, technically, Hoover's boss. During those years, the releases began: "U.S. Attorney General Robert F. Kennedy announced in Washington today..."

Those kinds of press releases usually include some stiff, wooden quotes from the boss that no respectable newspaper would print.

TV Is Pictures and Sound

Television is pictures, and sound.

Some major corporations are beginning to catch on. There is even a glimmer of understanding in a few governmental agencies. The modern news release is a broadcast-quality, three-quarter-inch videocassette, usually produced by a professional studio.

The VCR Press Release

Automobile crashes videotaped in laboratory safety tests are a good example of this kind of release. The tests take place over months, or years. Knowing that someday you may want television news coverage, you videotape the tests as you go along. When you're ready for publicity, you don't try to produce a television news story. You supply videotape copies of the crash tests, and make agency officials and engineers available for interviews. The television reporter puts the story together, incorporating some of the crash videotape while he or the engineers talk, voice-over.

When a new airliner makes its inaugural flight, the manufacturer supplies videotape of the plane's interior, the plane in flight, and on the assembly line.

Don't tell me. Show me.

Public Information Officers

Most companies and government agencies of any size now have at least one public information officer (PIO). Many of them grew up in newspapers and don't have the foggiest notion of how to deal with television.

The most common misuse occurs in police and fire departments where the chief designates the PIO as spokesperson for the entire department. No matter what happens, only the chief or the PIO will speak to the news media. So the PIO becomes an information relay. Every time it passes from one hand to another, the information becomes more stale and less personal. The chance for error multiplies.

He Doesn't Know How It Feels

Most important – the PIO wasn't there when it happened. He can't answer television's most pressing question.

A police officer is shot in the chest at close range. His only injury is a bad bruise. His bullet-proof vest saved him. Television wants to talk to him, not the PIO. TV wants pictures of the bruise. What is it like to be shot and live to tell about it?

The PIO's function *should be* to arrange those interviews. To make people available to camera crews at a convenient time and place. To arrange camera tours of crime and fire scenes, or manufacturing plants, or military bases. To be a walking directory that can lead reporters to the right place, the right people, the right information.

The PIO for a government agency and a private company should have different goals. Similar, but different.

In the private sector, part of the job involves putting the company's best foot forward. It is part public information, part public relations. Sometimes, it means hiding or disguising information that is unfavorable.

Public vs. Private

Too many public information officers in government fail to understand the perils if they adopt those same objectives. They think it is their job to make the boss, or the agency, look good. In doing that, they may stall, or try to block a reporter. They may fail to disclose something. Or lie to the media.

Nothing gives a reporter more incentive than the belief that you're hiding something. When the distortion or deception is uncovered, the agency will be damaged and the PIO may lose his job. On television, the lie can be played over and over again. (The news media seem far less critical of deceptive games when private industry plays them than when the players are government officials or employees.)

The primary purpose of the government PIO should be to act as an information conduit. He should know where information and resource people are, so he can guide the television crew there. At major news stories, he should coordinate media coverage so key people don't have to give the same interview 20 times.

Press Conferences: a Necessary Evil

Press conferences are a necessary evil.

Good reporters don't like them. Everybody will come away with the same story. Most reporters need to win. To beat the competition.

But press conferences are necessary. It would take all day to give individual interviews to four television stations, a dozen radio stations, and two newspapers. So you do them all at once for a major story. Television calls it a gang-bang. That's fairly descriptive of what reporters think of the process.

If you have to hold a press conference, choose the right time and place.

The Earlier, the Better

The earlier in the afternoon, the better. For a six o'clock newscast, three o'clock is about the absolute deadline. If you begin at three, the television crew may not be able to break down their gear and get away before four. A 30-minute drive back to the station gets the writing started at 4:30. Script finished and approved by 5:15 means only 45 minutes to edit, during the worst traffic jam of the day in the editing booths. If other stories are breaking late that day, your press conference may have a tough time competing.

In a crunch, a daily, 90-second news story can be slapped together in 15 minutes. But it looks like it. Since a press conference can be called at any time, the earlier you set it, the more care and attention the story will have.

The Right Place

Where you hold the press conference is also important. Most of them are set in big, bare rooms. It's sort of like eating at McDonald's. You've seen one, you've seen them all.

Think about the way television reporters shoot their standups. If the story involves a trial, we see the courthouse over the reporter's shoulder. Network correspondents who cover the president do their standups on the lawn of the White House. At space shots or political conventions we see the launch pad or the banners in the background. It is a kind of visual shorthand that television has developed. It says the reporter was actually there. It suggests that because he was there, he knows what he's talking about.

Show Me While You Talk

With a press conference, you can sometimes do the same thing. If you're an officer in the longshoremen's union, hold your press conference on the docks, so we can see the ships docked at the wharf behind you. If you're a military officer, have the tools of your trade in the background – a tank, a fighter plane, a submarine.

If you're a cop, talking about street crime, go to the most violent neighborhood in your community and talk about the problem on the street, where it happens.

Forget about prepared statements for press conferences. Reading them makes everybody snore. You may want to hand out fact sheets. Give reporters time to read them, so they can ask intelligent questions.

Another way to get your message across is to provide poster-sized graphics – charts, diagrams, maps – that the TV crew can shoot when the press conference ends. This will help tremendously to make the story more visually interesting.

Joint Press Conferences

Joint press conferences are a major logistical problem for television. The most common strings out five or six people at a long table, facing the cameras. It's often done to satisfy internal protocol and massage tender egos. Every agency that participated wants to be part of the glory.

The Sound Problem

The problem is: How do you arrange microphones so everybody can be heard? Unless you're in front of a mike, the videotape is useless. It's also difficult to swing the camera from one end of the table to the other and re-focus when someone else speaks.

The sound problem can be overcome, if each person participating has a microphone that feeds into a central sound system, and each broadcaster can plug into the sound system.

If you don't have a sophisticated sound system, the best solution is probably a podium for everybody's mike, with those participating in the conference standing close to the podium. Reporters can ask questions of specific people, and they can easily move to the mikes to answer. If they're seated, going back and forth from their chairs to the mike is a nightmare.

The Boss Doesn't Know Everything

Another important point — don't put some-body into a press conference solely because of his title. The boss may be the one to make a policy statement, but if it's details the media want, put the expert into the press conference who knows those details. It's embarrassing when the boss doesn't know the answer, fakes it, makes a mistake, and has to ask someone on his staff to correct his error. One way is to have both at the conference. The boss answers policy questions, then hands off to the staffer who's been personally involved with the detail work.

Careful with the Names

In a one-on-one interview, it's usually a good idea to use the reporter's name in your answers. "I've been doing this, Sally, because I think the school system is a disaster."

In a press conference, your recognizing one television reporter by name may prevent the competing stations from using your answer. That's how competitive they are.

Don't Leave Too Soon

When the press conference ends, don't leave too quickly. Some reporters who think they have something about the story all to themselves don't want to give away their scoop by asking you about it during the press conference.

The reporter who thinks he has an exclusive will want to get you aside, where other reporters can't hear, to question you on that angle. He may want to go back to your office with you for a private, on-camera interview.

Chapter 8

Wake Up the Photographer

It is a major speech. You know the media will be there. You *want* them to be there because the audience you need to reach is the entire community, far beyond the civic club or union hall and your live audience.

And so you spend a lot of time writing the speech. Polishing phrases. Trying them out on your co-workers.

The big day comes, and sure enough, there are three television cameras, their legs spread wide, standing directly in front of the platform. The bright lights come on as you're introduced, and you begin, with all the cameras rolling.

But the beginning is jokes and fluff. By the time you reach the heart of the speech, the lights are dark and the cameras dead. The photographers are back at their seats, eating their pie. Or dozing.

Speeches are like winding rivers. There's often no way to tell when you'll come around the bend into rapids and white water. When you get to that point, the reporter will nudge the photographer, wake him up, and get the videotape rolling again. But by the time the camera is fired up, you may be back into calm water. The photographer shrugs his shoulders and goes back to his pie.

You may interrupt his dessert several times. The real message may never reach the television audience.

Don't let it happen next time. Here's how to make sure the photographer will be awake and rolling at the critical moment:

Release Advance Copies

Give copies of the speech in advance to every reporter there. This gives them an opportunity to read through and pick the sections they want to videotape.

Since they will only have air time to report your major thrust—perhaps one side issue—they will mark those sections, and tell the photographer to shoot them.

Back at the station, this saves editing time. They know exactly what they have on tape. It doesn't have to be logged, and they don't have to roll back and forth through long sections of dull tape, searching for a usable bite.

Leak Part of It

Leak portions of the speech to the morning newspaper the day before. This will work only if what you're saying is truly newsworthy. If it is, the morning paper will have a story:

"In a speech prepared for delivery at today's meeting of the Chum and Chowder Society, Power Company President Mike Megawatt says electric bills will rise much higher if his company is not allowed to burn coal in its Smoky Hollow plant."

The advance story in the newspaper convinces television assignment editors they should have a camera there to cover it. The newspaper will be there, also, to see what else happens. You might say something in the question-and-answer session following the speech. Or the audience might lynch you.

Leaking the speech gives you two newspaper stories for one speech; the newspaper alerts readers to watch for the story on television tonight; it convinces the TV assignment editor the speech is worth covering, and the advance story will probably turn out a bigger, more responsive audience.

IMPORTANT: Don't leak everything to the newspaper in advance. Save the best quotes. That way, your audience won't feel like they're hearing a second-hand speech. And there will be fresh material for tonight's newscast.

Signaling When the Speech Is Off-the-Cuff

Many of the best, most newsworthy speeches are not written in advance. Some are spontaneous, unrehearsed, never written at all. So you need to develop signals that tell the photographer you're approaching something worth taping.

You're moving along, and you know the exciting stuff is just around the corner. You look over and see the camera is idle. To wake up the photographer, give him a warning. Something like:

Listen Up, Now

● "Now, if you don't hear anything else I say today, I want you to hear this. This is important." Or:

● "What I'm about to say is going to make a lot of people angry. It's going to cause a lot of hard feelings."

You can hear the cameras clicking all over the room.

● "Before I came here today, I gave a lot of thought to what I'm about to say. Nobody else has been willing to say this in public. I think it's time we talked about it."

That kind of tease not only wakes up the photographer, it whets the appetite of your audience. It makes them sit up and pay attention, too.

Summarize

You may discover that the summary is the perfect form for television's time limitations. After every important section of a speech, either prepared or off-the-cuff, **summarize.**

Chapter 9

Ambush Interviews and Other Traps

It may happen one bright spring morning. You will have no warning, no inclination to be cautious. As you leave your house and unlock the car in the driveway, you probably will not notice the van parked halfway up the block. Even if you are wary, you will not see the hidden camera videotaping everything you do.

As you come out of the driveway, the van starts up and pulls away from the curb. It stays a discreet half-block behind as you drive to your office.

You drive to your usual parking spot, a block from your building. Again, you do not notice the same van, double-parked just ahead. As you walk past, two men jump out the rear door. You do not see them. One is carrying a videotape camera on his shoulder. The other, just behind, has the recorder and microphone. They are wired together by the umbilical cable connecting camera and recorder. They come at a trot, approaching from behind. You never hear them.

A reporter who thinks of himself as a young Mike Wallace, complete with trenchcoat, is leaning, unnoticed, against a building. The reporter steps out in front of you, blocking the sidewalk. At that instant, the camera crew bursts ahead. With a start, you see them for the first time. The reporter says, "Good morning, I'm Mike Wallet from Channel Seven. I'd like to talk to you about your company's financial problems."

A Difficult Time— No Matter How Cool

It is a difficult time, no matter how cool you are. The surprise of the camera crew is a jolt. You look frightened. Your pulse is racing. Your breathing is short and hard. You have only a fraction of a second to decide what you will do. You may not make a conscious decision. You may act reflexively.

Some of your options:

1. **Punch out the reporter,** swing your briefcase at the camera, and run like crazy to get away from them.

2. **Keep walking,** but duck your head and put your hand in front of the camera lens. The camera crew will stick with you, the reporter firing non-stop questions, on into the lobby, all the way up the elevator, into the reception area of your office. Somewhere along the way, you will probably utter a "No comment" as you grit your teeth and stare straight ahead.

3. **Stop dead in your tracks.** "I have no idea what you're talking about. Now if you'll excuse me, I have to get to work."

4. **Say: "Good morning, Mike.** Gee, if you want to talk to me, come on up and I'll see when I can squeeze you in today. If you'd called, I would have been glad to give you an appointment." In this scenario, the reporter will still keep the camera rolling, and fire questions all the way to the office. He is afraid you will not give him an appointment.

5. **Say: "I'll be very glad to give you an interview,** but let's talk first, off camera. If you're sincere in wanting to talk to me and not in making me look like some kind of criminal, turn the camera off right now, and come on up. I'll get us a cup of coffee."

Heads They Win, Tails You Lose

The ambush technique has been used, and abused, throughout the history of investigative reporting on television. Reporters know they can usually count on it to make the target of their story look bad. At the same time, they're carrying out their obligation to get your side of the issue. It's heads they win, tails you lose.

Some veteran reporters who have ambushed their targets for years are beginning to question the fairness of the technique. The audience has become more sophisticated. Part of the re-thinking involves their not wanting to look like a TV bully picking on a defenseless little guy. The audience believes television has enormous power. If reporters and camera crews abuse that power – if it appears they don't fight fair – the audience will side with the little guy. So more TV reporters are falling back on the ambush interview only as a last resort.

If They Want You, They'll Get You

Television is words and pictures – mostly pictures. If they are to write words about you, they must have your picture. Good investigative reporters take great pride in their persistence. If they truly want your picture, they will get it. Unless you lock yourself in a fallout shelter for the next year. Even then, there are ways to get to you, or get you out. So the only question is, what do you say when they catch up with you?

Let's go back and examine your options in an ambush.

1. **Punch out the reporter.** This makes great video. You can be sure every moment will be played on the air. At least three or four times. You will enhance your reputation as a hoodlum. Few people will side with you. They will decide you are guilty, as charged. If there is another side to the story, it won't be told. The reporter can have you arrested for assault and

battery. He has excellent grounds for a civil suit. The proof for either criminal or civil action is all on videotape. You will probably boost the reporter's career immeasurably.

2. **Refuse to talk, keep walking.** In most cases, this will also make you look like a nasty guy with something to hide. Remember—television, like politics, is often a matter of impressions, not exact words.

3. **"Excuse me, I have to get to work."** Here, you've said *something*. The audience knows you're human. But you're still cold, elusive, probably guilty. This option has many modifications. If you don't want to give a full interview or answer questions, you can take this opportunity to get at least a brief statement on the air. "No comment" is like taking the Fifth Amendment. Many people will assume you're guilty. Otherwise, why not talk to the reporter? You need to explain.

His question has suggested there are financial problems in your company. You can say something like, "We've become aware of a cash flow problem in the last week or so, and we're working on it. The company is not in danger. We're negotiating now with some new investors, and that is a delicate thing. I really can't say very much about it. If you'll give me your name and phone number, I'll be glad to call you when we come to an agreement."

This answer will guarantee a string of questions, that you can politely refuse to answer, giving your reason for declining. You may want to answer some of them.

4. **Make an interview appointment.** If you're polite, the reporter tends to return the courtesy. In making the appointment, try to

find out as much as you can about the story he's working on. You may have to do some research to answer some of the questions. Delaying the interview for several hours will give you time to be better prepared.

5. **"Let's talk first, off-camera."** This is probably the best choice if you're concerned about getting a fair shake from the reporter. News people work a lot on instinct. From experience, they tend to be suspicious. Anything you do that appears to evade, to delay, to deceive or cover up will feed their suspicion and probably will be reflected in their copy.

Lay It All Out

During that off-camera talk, if you're not guilty, lay all your cards on the table. That may be the end of the interview, and the story. The off-camera interview gives you a better opportunity to fully explain your side of the issue. The reporter may not have all the facts from the other side. Collect documents and bring in staff, if that's necessary for a full presentation.

There is another element of self-defense that you should keep in mind. If you are a public person (we'll go into that in more detail later), you cannot collect in a libel suit unless the reporter broadcasts something false about you *knowing it is false.* If he broadcasts it, believing it is true, after taking reasonable care to prove it true, you cannot win a libel action.

You must not only prove it was false—you must prove the reporter did a sloppy job; had information showing the story was false, but ignored it.

Keeping the Reporter Honest

If you are concerned about the integrity of the reporter, it might be a good idea to have a witness present while you make your case. Get a receipt for any documents you provide. And during the on-camera interview, make your own audio recording of the entire interview. Let the reporter know you're recording it.

If, in asking for the off-camera interview, you said you'd talk on camera, don't back out. If you'll lie about giving an interview, surely you'll lie about more important things. Reporters are always afraid to delay on-camera interviews. Too many people change their minds.

The Camera Is a Lie Detector

Remember: The camera is an excellent lie detector. Like the polygraph, it can sometimes be fooled. But if you're caught in an on-camera lie, television will never forget. It will be played over and over again. You can't say you were misquoted. The lie is there, on tape, to haunt you forever.

The audience is also smart enough to know when you're evading a question. In most cases, it's probably better to say you can't answer than to evade the question.

A good reporter, like a good courtroom lawyer, never asks a question unless he already knows the answer.

Deciding whether to talk to an investigative reporter is very complex unless the charges he is pursuing are absolutely false.

If he has been misled — if he has drawn an understandably false conclusion from the evidence — then you should talk to him.

Not Guilty: A True Investigative Story

A real-life example:

An anonymous caller tells a reporter he should investigate why the Urban Renewal Agency paid the city attorney twice as much for his house as it paid the owners of other identical houses on the same block. The reporter goes to property records at the courthouse and discovers the tip is accurate. The lots on the block are all the same size. The houses are all similar, built at the same time, and have been carried on the tax assessor's rolls at virtually the same value. Yet when the Urban Renewal Agency bought the entire block, it paid the city attorney, with good political connections, twice as much as anybody else. Apparently an open-and-shut case.

The reporter goes to the city attorney, his last step before broadcasting the story.

"Yeah, they paid me twice as much," the city attorney says. "But I didn't keep the money. You see, I had leased the house to a color photo processing company. The lease said if they ever had to move for any reason during the term of the lease, I would have to pay for their relocation and build them another processing plant. I've got a copy of the lease in my file, if you'd like to read it."

Oh. I see. Three days of research down the tubes. No story.

When You've Goofed

If the story the reporter is pursuing involves your making an honest mistake, it's probably in your best interest to say so.

Richard Nixon would have been a very different figure in history if he had gone on television shortly after the Watergate burglars were caught to announce that someone at Republican Headquarters had made a dreadful mistake; that he, as the party nominee, would accept the blame and see that those responsible were brought to justice.

Long after he had resigned in disgrace, Nixon consented to a series of televised interviews with David Frost. The most emotional moment in those hours of conversation came when Frost told Nixon he wished the fallen president could admit that he made a mistake in trying to cover up the break-in. Nixon stonewalled. Frost tried again, almost begging Nixon to confess and ask forgiveness. The cameras were close, flicking from Frost to Nixon, then Frost, and back again. You could almost hear Richard Nixon's heart pounding. It was like that moment in the revival tent when everybody is singing and praying that the town sinner in the back row will walk down the aisle to repent and be saved.

After a heavy pause that seemed forever, Nixon said he had done nothing to be sorry for, and turned away.

When You're on Trial

Past the point of admitting an honest mistake, the decision on whether to be interviewed on camera gets stickier. It depends on how serious the accusation, and your involvement in it. In a sense, you are on trial. The reporter will present the charges, and the evidence against you, to the audience/jury. If the defense decides to rest with no evidence, no witnesses, we have been conditioned to believe that is a concession of guilt.

It's Hard To Con a TV Camera

Looking guilty by refusing to talk to a reporter may be better than taking the stand and convincing the audience you're not only guilty, you're a liar as well. Career con men often amaze reporters by agreeing to a sit-down interview. It is a heady challenge, to see if they can out-smart, out-talk the reporter. They rarely win.

If there are people and documents that support your side of the controversy, the reporter may not know about them unless you tell him. Refusing to talk to him will almost always insure a one-sided story.

What Are You Hiding?

It's hard to draw lines for every situation. But generally, reporters believe people who try to keep them out of offices, or meetings, or records have something to hide. The more open you can be with a reporter, the more open and fair he tends to be with you.

Remember – whatever the reporter does that is sneaky, or belligerent, whatever he does that might raise eyebrows, will be edited out before the story is broadcast. Anything you do that is less than flattering will be preserved for all the world to see.

Sneaking In

There are other kinds of surprises television reporters spring. They call and ask permission to shoot videotape in your business or office. "Just general footage to go with a story we're doing." Once inside, you discover they have quite another mission, and have entered by subterfuge.

Questions from Nowhere

Or, in the middle of what you thought would be a friendly interview, the reporter gets nasty. Springs a completely different subject on you. A sort of verbal ambush.

"Didn't your department fire four women in 1975 simply because they were pregnant?" the reporter snarls. You may not have the foggiest idea.

Too often, people who don't know the answer to a question answer it anyhow, saying what they assume or hope is accurate. Later, when it turns out they're wrong, it looks like they were lying or trying to cover up. If you don't know, say so. And tell the reporter you'll get the answer.

Chapter 10

Fairness and Equal Time

"Congress shall make no law respecting an establishment of religion, or prohibiting the free exercise thereof; or abridging the freedom of speech or of the press; or the right of the people peaceably to assemble, and to petition the government for a redress of grievances."

The First Amendment to the U.S. Constitution is a simple, straightforward statement. *Congress shall make no law* abridging freedom of speech or press.

No weasel words. No loopholes for lawyers to play with.

Yet for more than half a century, Congress has made laws, and created agencies to regulate broadcasters. To tell them what they can — and cannot — say on the air. The laws give government the power to take away a broadcaster's license if he doesn't follow the rules. And all this has been given the blessing of the U.S. Supreme Court.

Most people in America now get their news from television. The government's regulation of television seems a strange contradiction in a nation that preaches press freedom as a basic requirement for democracy.

How Did We Get from There to Here?

As AM radio spread across the world in the 1920s, the broadcast band became crowded. Radio signals began to override each other, much like the spread of the CB radio in the 1970s. An investor in a radio station in 1925 quickly discovered nobody could hear what he was broadcasting. If another station within a hundred miles was using the same frequency, everything was garbled. At that time, you were completely free to broadcast on any frequency at any power level you chose. As the

106

number of stations grew, finding a clear channel became more and more difficult. Even if you found one, there was no guarantee it would stay clear very long.

Getting Around the First Amendment

Broadcasters went to Washington to solve the problem. Their lawyers came up with a theory that would get around the First Amendment and allow Congress to regulate the industry.

It goes something like this: Radio waves cross state lines. Therefore, broadcasting is interstate commerce. The Constitution gives Congress the right to regulate interstate commerce.

The Public Sky

Of course, newspapers cross state lines, too. So a second argument was devised. Broadcasters do not own the medium that carries their signal – the sky. Radio waves must go through the sky. The sky belongs to the public. Therefore, the public has a right to regulate how its sky is used.

1927– the FRC

In 1927, Congress created the Federal Radio Commission to regulate all broadcasting in America. The commission was to give order and decency to the airwaves. Anybody using the public sky had to get a license. The commission decided who was fit to hold a license.

1934 – the FCC

In 1934, Congress rewrote the Radio Act and created today's Federal Communications Commission. There was no question that Congress, through the FCC, restricted freedom of both speech and the press. Most people

accepted it as a practical, though unconstitu-
tional solution to a technical problem. Either
you regulate broadcasting, or nobody will be
able to broadcast. Simple as that.

Shortly after it was created, the old Radio
Commission began to regulate not only the
signals and equipment broadcasters used, but
what they said over the air, and how they allo-
cated their time.

Licensing radio stations created an immediate political problem. In many towns, there
was only one station. In a political campaign,
the owner could use his station to help one
side and hurt — or ignore — the other. Equal
Time and the Fairness Doctrine were born.

Only Politicians Get Equal Time

Many people confuse fairness and equal
time. If a television story criticizes them or
their business, they demand equal time to reply. Only politicians get equal time. Congress,
in its wisdom, made it that way.

If a station gives air time to a politician during a campaign, it must give equal time to his
opponent. If the station runs an editorial en-
dorsing a candidate or an issue, it must give
equal time to the other side — or sides.

To carry out the pretense of press freedom,
the Equal Time law has a clause exempting
news coverage. The same kind of convoluted
reasoning that enabled Congress to waltz
around the First Amendment can also take
Equal Time for a spin.

Presidential Debates and Equal Time

In 1960, after Richard Nixon and John F.
Kennedy agreed to a series of nationally televised debates, Congress passed a special suspension of Equal Time requirements for that

year's presidential campaign so every candidate wouldn't have to be included.

The question came up again in 1976, when the networks planned a series of debates between challenger Jimmy Carter and incumbent Gerald Ford. Both agreed to participate. Everything was all set. Then Cong. Shirley Chisolm, also a candidate for president, demanded that she be included. The law seemed to be on her side. Without another congressional suspension, if you give Carter and Ford air time to debate, you have to put Chisolm on the platform and on the networks. There were other, more obscure candidates out there, too, who would all get equal time. Candidates for the Socialist Party, the Prohibition Party, the Vegetarian Party — you name it, there's a candidate out there for it somewhere, and they all get equal network time.

The networks called their lawyers. What do we do now? A debate between a dozen candidates will be a zoo. Nobody will watch. It will run all night.

Bending the Law

Some legal contortionist came forward with the solution.

The networks decided to cancel the debate. Forget the whole thing.

Then the League of Women Voters announced it would sponsor a debate between Jimmy Carter and Gerald Ford. The League made it clear that Chisolm and all those other tag-along candidates would not be included. Equal Time laws don't apply to the League of Women Voters.

Aha! the networks said. If you sponsor a debate between the two major candidates, it will be a news event, and we'll cover it.

Chisolm v. Federal Communications Commission, 538 F.2d 349 [D.C.Circ.] (1976)

Chisolm and the National Organization for Women ran to the FCC. The FCC announced it had been misinterpreting Congress' intent all those years in requiring equal time for all candidates if debates were broadcast. If the League of Women Voters wanted to invite two candidates to debate, and the networks covered it as a bona fide news event, then Equal Time did not apply, the FCC decided.

Chisolm and NOW took the FCC decision to court. They lost. A panel of U.S. Circuit judges agreed with the FCC's new policy. Government can't make news judgments for broadcasters, the court decided. The U.S. Supreme Court refused to hear an appeal. The debate was televised, just as originally planned with only Carter and Ford on the platform.

Newspapers Are Different

Compare television's equal time requirement with an almost exact parallel in the print media.

In 1913, the Florida legislature passed a law protecting the election process from unfair newspaper influence. It was introduced by a lawmaker who was a newspaperman and signed by a governor who was a newspaper publisher. It said that candidates had the right to reply to newspaper attacks during a political campaign. Before the election, the newspaper had to give equal space to the other side, and print it in the same general section of the newspaper.

It is the fall of 1972, and the Florida Equal Space Law has never been seriously challenged. Pat Tornillo, leader of the teachers' union in Miami, is running for the Florida legislature.

Tornillo and the editor of the *Miami Herald* are old enemies. The *Herald* is a dominant newspaper that, even today, does not have a single union anywhere in its operation. Its editorial page will almost always side with management and against unions. The animosity between the *Herald* editor and Tornillo had become much more personal and intense in 1968, when Tornillo led a teachers' strike the *Herald* felt was illegal.

Hydrofoils and Hoopla

Tornillo is a flamboyant, clever strategist with an eye for the grand gesture. During that 1968 strike, he had rented a stadium on Biscayne Bay for teacher rallies. Tornillo would roar up to the floating platform in a rented hydrofoil to the applause of his followers.

So it is 1972, four years later, and Tornillo has his eye on the state capitol. The *Herald* opposes him with two scathing editorials:

> *"The screeds say the strike is not an issue. We say maybe it wouldn't be were it not a part of a continuation of disregard of any and all laws the Classroom Teachers' Association might find aggravating. ...What's good for CTA is good for CTA and that is natural law. Tornillo's law, maybe. For years now he has been kicking the public shin to call attention to his shakedown statesmanship. He and whichever acerbic prexy is in alleged office have always felt their private ventures so chock-full of public weal that we should leap at the chance to nab the tab, be it half the Glorious Leader's salary or the dues checkoff or*

anything else except perhaps mileage on the staff hydrofoil. Give him public office, says Pat, and he will no doubt live by the Golden Rule. Our translation reads that as more gold and more rule."

So Pat Tornillo and his lawyer go to the *Herald* to demand equal space to reply. The *Herald* tells him to jump in the bay.

Tornillo Wins at First

Tornillo goes to court to force the *Herald* to comply with the 1913 law. Meanwhile Tornillo loses his campaign for the legislature. The Florida Supreme Court sides with Tornillo. The justices there decide that equal space is not a violation of the First Amendment. After all, they note, federal law gives candidates equal time to reply on the airwaves. The Florida decision quotes heavily from the U.S. Supreme Court opinion that had upheld the FCC's Fairness Doctrine and government's right to regulate what broadcasters put on the air.

The *Herald* is not about to lie down and take Tornillo's victory in the state supreme court. The newspaper appeals to the U.S. Supreme Court.

The Supreme Court's Opinion

This time, Tornillo and Florida's Equal Space Law lose. Writing the opinion for a unanimous court in June, 1974, Chief Justice Warren Burger says:

"The issue in this case is whether a state statute granting a political candidate a right to equal space to reply to criticisms and attacks on his record by a newspaper violates the guarantee of a free press. ...The choice

of material to go into a newspaper...
whether fair or unfair — constitutes
exercise of editorial control and judg-
ment. It has yet to be demonstrated
how governmental regulation of this
crucial process can be exercised con-
sistent with First Amendment guar-
antees of a free press."

The Press Is Not TV

Miami Herald
Publishing Co.
v. Tornillo,
418 U.S. 241,
94 S.Ct. 2831,
41 L.Ed.2d. 730
(1974)

In his opinion striking down all equal space laws, the Chief Justice does not mention the court's very different attitude about equal time and the regulation of broadcast journalism. To justify that regulation, the court had decided years earlier that electronic media are not "The Press" the framers of the Constitution had in mind when they wrote the First Amendment.

Justice White, writing a concurring opinion in the Tornillo case, reflects that difference of attitude when he says:

> *"The First Amendment erects a*
> *virtually insurmountable barrier*
> *between government and the* print
> *media."* (Emphasis added.)

Equal time, as you've seen, is a very narrow concept, applied only to political issues and candidates.

The Fairness Doctrine

The Fairness Doctrine is a much broader concept adopted by the FCC and incorporated into federal law. It says broadcasters must be fair in covering "controversial issues of public importance." Since the number of broadcast licensees is limited, the legal theory here says that television stations have an obligation to carry all points of view on those matters of "public importance."

Where Does It Say They Have To Be Fair?

This, again, is a radical departure from the way the printed press has operated in this country. There has never been any legal obligation for newspapers to be fair. The early journalists in this country were revolutionary philosophers — zealots who used their printing presses to spread politics and religion. Their stories were grossly distorted to make their friends appear saintly and their enemies, grotesque. Until early in this century, most newspapers announced their political bias on their front pages or mastheads. You didn't need to look at their declaration of political point of view. You knew, from reading their stories, they were Whigs or Tories, Republicans or Populists.

The Economics of Fairness

Economic pressure forced newspapers to be more fair. The early crusading newspaper editors had been much more interested in their causes than in their credit ratings. Their papers were sometimes distributed free, to a small group of readers who usually agreed with the editor's point of view. The more outrageous the editor's attack on his enemies, the better his readers liked it.

Occasionally, the early papers entertained. But primarily, they printed ideas and information, often without hoping to make a profit. It was a labor of love and ego, conscience and politics.

Advertising's Calming Influence

As advertising became an accepted part of daily and weekly newspapers, the stories were toned down. It was important not to alienate large sections of advertisers, or the readers advertisers paid to reach. The mass circulation dailies in the early 1900s were not exactly fair — but the sensational stories that became the battleground for the circulation wars were unfair only to truth and the small group of people they wrote about — the people unfortunate enough to be caught in the crossfire.

Justice White, in that same concurring Tornillo opinion, said:

> *"Of course, the press is not always accurate, or even responsible, and may not present full and fair debate on important public issues. But the balance struck by the First Amendment with respect to the press is that society must take the risk that occasionally debate on vital matters will not be comprehensive and that all viewpoints may not be expressed. The press would be unlicensed because, in Jefferson's words, 'where the press is free, and every man able to read, all is safe.' Any other accommodation – any other system that would supplant private control of the press with the heavy hand of government intrusion – would make the government the censor of what the people may read and know."*

TV – a Different Heritage

The heritage for broadcasting is very different. From the beginning, television was conceived as an entertainment medium. For most decisions, the highest priority was profit. Television also depended on a large audience. Fear of offending that audience, and the chilling effect of government looking over their shoul-

115

ders, made most television outlets shy away from anything even slightly controversial.

Conflict in the streets made good film, but few stations took the risk of saying anything editorially about that conflict. Edward R. Murrow became a legend because he was willing to tackle subjects like Sen. Joseph McCarthy's witch hunt for communists, and the abuse of migrant farm labor.

News was – and still is – a small fraction of television's programming day. Until September, 1963, network news totalled 15 minutes per day – including commercials. The entire news staff at many local stations was one man who served as reporter, photographer and anchorman.

An Acquired Taste

The public's thirst for news is an acquired taste. In the early 1970s, staff at CBS's "60 Minutes" constantly kept feelers out for other jobs. Whether the program could survive with such low ratings was questionable. Ten years later, it became the most-watched show in the country.

Still, there is that specter of somebody at the FCC watching, playing referee, deciding what is fair and unfair.

Early in this decade, the FCC relinquished some of its power to regulate radio. There is a move now to do the same with television. Technology has opened up so many broadcast channels now, almost everybody who wants to broadcast can find a station or a cable channel. The old argument to justify government regulation is no longer valid.

Until television is deregulated, however, the Fairness Doctrine stands. Courts interpreting what it means have decided fairness does not require equal time.

How Do You Measure Fairness?

One of the best interpretations of fairness is a U.S. Circuit Court opinion written in the District of Columbia in 1974. The case involved an NBC documentary narrated by Edwin Newman, "Pensions: the Broken Promise."

Accuracy in Media — a group concerned with the growing power of the press — filed a formal complaint with the FCC, saying, "The NBC report gave the viewers a grotesquely distorted picture of the private pension system of the United States."

The FCC ruled NBC had not lived up to its fairness obligation and ordered more air time for opposing views. NBC challenged the FCC ruling in court.

"Pensions: the Broken Promise"

The documentary shows a series of old people, who had worked for a company most of their lives, looking forward to retirement and their pensions. In each of the personal stories, the pension was never paid. Some companies went bankrupt, and there was no money for pensions. Some workers moved from one union to another, not realizing they lost benefits when they transferred. In some cases, the companies simply fired workers shortly before they were eligible to draw their pensions.

The appellate court ruled that Newman and NBC *had* met the Fairness Doctrine requirements. A broadcast report, the court said, does not have to give equal time and attention to every part of its subject. It must focus on the unusual — the newsworthy — the court said, quoting from a memo that had been filed

117

in the case by the American Society of Newspapers:

> *"Newspapers investigate and expose policemen who are on the 'take' in the dope rackets. If equivalent time must be given to policemen who are not on the 'take' the whole campaign becomes so unwieldy and pointless as to be useless."*

National Broadcasting Co., Inc. v. FCC, 516 F.2d 1101 [D.C.Circ.] (1974)

The judges who ruled in favor of NBC were impressed with the two-minute monologue that closed the documentary. In it, the court said, Newman met the fairness standard. The decision quotes it in full:

> *NEWMAN: "This has been a depressing program to work on, but we don't want to give the impression that there are no good private pension plans. There are many good ones, and there are many people for whom the promise has become reality. That should be said."*

Newman summed up all the problems the program had explored, and then concluded:

> *"These are matters for Congress to consider and, indeed, the Senate Labor Committee is considering them now. They are also matters for those who are in pension plans. If you're in one, you might find it useful to take a close look at it. Our own conclusion about all of this is that it is almost inconceivable that this enormous thing has been allowed to grow up with so little understanding of it and with so little protection and such un-*

even results for those involved. The situation, as we've seen it, is deplorable. Edwin Newman, NBC News."

Fairness: in the Eye of the Beholder

Fairness is very much like beauty. It is in the eye of the beholder. Politics can cloud that eye. Television has grown less afraid of FCC censure in recent years. But that could change.

Public censure has become a more realistic threat to keep television news honest and fair. The audience has developed its own sense of how the game is played, and what is expected in terms of fairness. The media are more willing to report on each other — to embarrass their competition when they go outside the bounds of good taste or accepted standards.

If you feel you've been treated unfairly, we'll tell you where and how to complain later.

Chapter 11

Can They Do That and Get Away with It?

It depends on who you are, as well as what they show and tell. No matter how powerful television seems to be, there usually are ways to get even if a broadcast damages you unjustly.

Sue. For libel, or invasion of privacy. The jury might make you a millionaire.

But before you rush to the courthouse, you should know what you're getting into. Collecting damages can take years. You'll need a very good attorney, because this area of law is complicated. It's still evolving. The television station or network will have on its side some of the best legal counsel available. If your suit has no merit, the judge might make you pay the attorneys' fees for the other side when he dismisses it.

Don't expect a quick settlement. Many major publishing and broadcasting firms have a policy of never settling out of court. Settlements tend to encourage other suits. In the long run, it's cheaper to fight to the bitter end – and lose – than to put up with the hassle of a new lawsuit every week.

Your Life Will Be an Open Book

Once you file suit, you open your entire life. If there is anything in your past that could be embarrassing or painful, it will almost surely be found and publicized. One of the best defenses in a civil suit is a good offense. Your suit will give the broadcaster subpoena power to get records, and drag in witnesses who must testify under oath. They will explore everything about your finances, your family, your medical history, your professional career, your education and your sex life.

Still want to sue? OK. Let's look at the two areas of law. They're similar in some respects, but also very different.

In matters of governmental regulation (see Chapter Ten), the courts have treated newspapers and broadcasting differently. In libel and privacy, the courts make few distinctions between print and broadcast.

Libel

You have been libeled if a publication or broadcast unjustifiably damages you. If your friends, your family, the people at work or the club think less of you after they see the story, you have evidence of your damage. The people who see the report don't have to know you for it to damage your reputation.

The story can hurt you financially, by decreasing your future income. It can damage you emotionally, by causing embarrassment, ridicule and anguish.

Television stories probably libel hundreds of people every day in America, yet few suits are filed. The law provides several defenses for the media, based on freedom of press and speech.

Defense #1: Truth

The law says they can libel you and get away with it if the story is true. Truth is an almost perfect defense in a libel suit.

How do you prove something is true? How many witnesses does it take, what kind of evidence?

There are no rigid rules. **Truth is what a jury will believe.**

A dozen prostitutes and pimps testify you were in their place of business every Sunday morning at 11 o'clock. Your priest says you never missed 11 o'clock Mass on Sunday morning. The jury will probably believe the priest, even though the witness score is 12-1.

Relaying the Libel

A broadcaster does not have to initiate the libel. If he passes on something someone else says about you, the station or network generally assumes responsibility for the truth of that statement.

Suppose you fire one of your employees. He then holds a press conference and says you are a drug smuggler who regularly encourages teenage employees to use cocaine and participate in sex orgies. A television station covers the press conference and reports what the disgruntled employee says about you.

It is *true* that he said it. But that will not protect the broadcaster who reports only what the employee says. The damaging information must be true. If the station acts as a relay for the employee's accusations, it must be prepared to prove to a jury that you are, indeed, a drug smuggler who encourages teenage employees to use cocaine and participate in sex orgies. If it convinces a jury that you do those things, then you cannot win a libel suit, no matter how much damage has been done to your reputation.

Defense #2: Privilege

If the damaging information comes from a part of the governmental process, the press has limited responsibility for the truth of that information. This is called privilege.

The legal theory says government officials should be able to do their jobs freely, without having to worry about libel suits. A Supreme Court justice once said freedom of speech does not give you the right to yell "Fire!" in a crowded theater when there is no fire. But a congressman can run up and down the aisles of the Capitol yelling "Fire!" — or anything else he chooses — without fear of reprisal. And in

a free society, the public needs to know —
through the news media — what its public
officials are doing and saying.

But It's Not True

Suppose that during a debate in the Senate
Chamber, a U.S. senator announces that you
murdered hundreds at Auschwitz. The story is
broadcast. As a result, you lose your job. An
angry crowd sets fire to your house. Your children are beaten on their way to school.

What the senator said was absolutely false.
But you cannot sue him. And you cannot win
a libel suit against the press for publishing
or broadcasting what the senator said. It is
privileged.

If you are charged with a crime, anything in
the criminal justice system records — part of
the governmental process — is privileged. Anything in a court suit — the testimony of a witness at a trial, the contents of a governmental
audit, what a policeman says during the
investigation of a crime — will almost always
be privileged.

Notice as we go through this chapter how
often we hedge with qualifiers like probably —
almost always — generally — usually. The rules
are not firm. They can be bent — and often
are — by judges and juries who feel they should
cure an injustice.

Most judges would probably extend privilege to what is said in political campaigns, or
presidential press conferences, even though
they are not part of the governmental process.

Defense #3: Absence of Malice

It is the early 1960s. Martin Luther King is
waging war against racial segregation in Alabama. He moves from city to city, encouraging
black followers to break the law. Use segregated

rest rooms, he tells them. Sit in segregated sections of the bus. Enter restaurants and hotels that bar blacks. King knows that if the law is bad, the only way it will be changed will be to make public officials enforce the bad law. His movement becomes a major national story. The police who enforce the law become the villains in that story as they use clubs, fire hoses, attack dogs and tear gas to drive back the demonstrators.

King learns how to use the media in his campaign. A committee goes to the *New York Times* and pays for a full-page ad attacking the public officials in Montgomery who lead the segregationist forces. The *New York Times* publishes the ad without checking its accuracy. As it turns out, some of the charges are not true.

New York Times Co. v. Sullivan,
376 U.S.254,
84 S.Ct.710,
11 L.Ed.2d 686
(1964)

The Alabama officials sue the *New York Times* for libel. In Montgomery, a jury of their peers finds the *New York Times* has, indeed, libeled those public servants and must be punished by paying them damages.

The *New York Times* appeals the verdict all the way to the U.S. Supreme Court. In 1964, *New York Times vs. Sullivan* makes new libel law for the nation. The press cannot be held responsible for the libel of a public official, the Supreme Court says, unless it publishes the libel with malice in its heart, knowing the information is false. The press must be found guilty of reckless disregard for truth before a public official can collect for libel, the court says.

In their decision, the justices acknowledge that many public officials will be damaged by untrue, libelous stories as this new ruling is applied. But the democratic process demands full and free debate – continuous open season on public officials – the court says. The public must be able to hear every accusation thrown at those in public office, and decide for itself whether that person deserves a position of public trust. If you can't take the political heat, stay out of the kitchen, the court warns.

What Is Reckless Disregard for Truth?

How far must a reporter go to check out damaging information about a public official to meet the absence of malice test? That's up to a judge or jury. In *New York Times vs. Sullivan,* the Supreme Court felt the *Times* had no obligation to check the accuracy of the paid advertisement.

Suppose the mayor has been waging war against local adult book stores and pornographic movies. He has a reputation as Mr. Clean. His campaign has pushed the X-rated shops into the suburbs, where city police have no jurisdiction. An anonymous caller tells a reporter the real motive for the mayor's crusade: Mr. Clean has a hidden financial interest in the shops that are opening up outside the city.

To be fair, the reporter asks the mayor if the charge is true. He gets an angry denial, and then runs a story that says, "Our sources tell us the real reason for the mayor's crusade. He holds a financial interest in the new chain of porno shops that have opened just outside the city limits. The mayor denies it."

Reckless disregard for truth? Almost certainly. If the only evidence is an anonymous tip, most juries will say the reporter and his station were reckless with the truth, and should be punished by paying damages to the mayor.

But suppose the reporter finds two prostitutes who say, on camera, that the mayor told them he secretly owns the massage parlor where they work? The outcome of a libel suit may now depend on the skill of the opposing attorneys.

Defense #3A: Public Persons

Back to the civil rights movement. As integration spreads across the South under court edicts and the muzzles of army rifles, a federal court orders the University of Mississippi to admit its first black student. He is escorted to the campus by a squad of U.S. marshals. That night, the marshals and a small army of reporters are driven into the university administration building by an angry mob. As the night wears on, the administration building comes under attack. The mob begins to shoot at the marshals and the building. Small groups charge, carrying Confederate flags, trying to break in. The federal government is once again in a shooting war with the rebellious South.

The Truth Battle at Oxford, Miss.

In the heat of the battle, someone runs into the Associated Press office and says a famous general is leading the charges at the Old Miss administration building – former U.S. Army General Edwin Walker. A bulletin is quickly typed. The story goes over the wire. It is published all over the world the next day.

General Walker had been a career soldier who believed strongly in the communist threat to America. As commander of U.S. forces in Europe, he had recommended that his troops read the John Birch Society's Blue Book, which accused former President Dwight D. Eisenhower and other national leaders of being communist dupes. Walker was relieved of his command. He retired and went on the lecture circuit. The wire services transmitted a picture of the general, flying an American flag upside down as a distress signal that the country was in trouble. He was a big enough celebrity that Lee Harvey Oswald took a shot at him. Oswald missed, then went on to Dallas.

Associated Press v. Walker, 388 U.S. 130, 87 S.Ct. 1975, 18 L.Ed. 2d 1094 (1967)

So the AP reports this famous general is leading the charge against the U.S. marshals. Walker sues for libel. The AP cannot trace the source of its information. It cannot prove that Walker was even on the campus that night. Walker wins the libel suit.

The AP appeals, and again the U.S. Supreme Court reverses. In 1967, the court extends the *New York Times vs. Sullivan* guidelines to "public persons." Public persons, like public officials, cannot win a libel judgment, the court rules, unless the press shows reckless disregard for truth.

In the heat and stress of the battle situation that night on the university campus, the court decides, the AP cannot be penalized for making an honest mistake.

Now you can understand why the tabloids are devoted to public officials and entertainers. The libel rules are much more lenient for public people. The press doesn't have to be absolutely sure the story is true, so long as they don't know it's false.

But the present Supreme Court seems more and more uneasy with that broad libel immunity. Later decisions have muddied the guidelines. Juries, too — as in the Carol Burnett case against the *National Enquirer* — sometimes try to re-draw the line.

Defense #4: Fair Comment

British law developed another area where the press could libel people and get away with it — theater critics. If a critic says an actor's performance is shoddy, and the script miserable, the review does great damage to everyone involved with the play. Not just their reputations — their livelihood. Some critics have the ability to shut down a play within days if they give it a bad review. Their opinions are as devastating as any false statement of fact.

Yet the law recognizes that different people are entitled to express different opinions. If you go on stage to display yourself in public, journalists have the right to throw figurative tomatoes if they don't like what they see. That same kind of license has been extended now to journalists who test cars, rate restaurants, or review other kinds of consumer services and products.

A damaging story can kill a new business. A favorable story, in the right place, can make millions for a new product.

There are *some* restrictions. Most courts would rule that the journalist who sets himself up as a judge of artistic or engineering merit can be successfully sued for libel if he misstates the facts in his review.

Privacy Invasion

In the next decade, the majority of suits against the media will probably claim invasion of privacy, not libel. Because of its cameras, lights and microphones, television is much more intrusive than print. Jurors have strong feelings about their own personal privacy, and privacy law — at this point — does not have as many exceptions as libel.

Privacy verdicts — even more than those in libel suits, depend on how the jury feels about the circumstances in each case. Personal privacy is a new legal concept in this country that is still developing.

The Bill of Rights protects citizens against unreasonable search and seizure. But that is a protection from government abuse, not private enterprise, or individuals. We inherited criminal trespass from British Common Law, but the idea of a right to privacy in your personal life was not conceived until the 1890s.

In the 1950s, electronics leaped far ahead of the old laws regulating wiretaps. A comprehensive federal statute to protect the privacy of conversation was not adopted until 1968. There still is no statutory privacy protection from a telephoto lens.

Trespass   Trespass is physical intrusion onto your property. It is a criminal act.

Invasion of privacy by a television crew can occur when they broadcast what they saw and heard while they were trespassing. The effect of the broadcast is to bring thousands —perhaps millions— of people into your home or business, where they have no right to be. Since you can't prosecute all of them (you don't even know who they are), a suit provides a way to financially punish the television outlet that ushered those hordes of people through your private property.

Shooting the videotape, and broadcasting it, are two different kinds of intrusion. If the tape is never shown to anybody else, then a simple trespass took place. Once the tape is played for others, the trespasser has brought other people inside your space, invading your privacy.

An invasion of privacy can also occur without physical trespass, if a broadcaster tells the world something about your life that is very intimate.

Let's go back now to trespass – physical intrusion – and work forward to the latest electronic eavesdropping devices.

Where TV Cameras Can Go

A television crew has the same freedom of movement as anyone else. If you can walk down the sidewalk, so can a television crew. We have public places in this society where anyone can go, unless a state of emergency is declared – streets, parks, subways, beaches, public buildings.

We sometimes give the press special access so they can represent the public and report what happens. At a major trial, for instance, seats are reserved for the media and some spectators are shut out. Reporters and photographers are allowed beyond police lines at disasters so they can see, record and photograph the victims and the rescue effort.

There are some public places where citizens have access but cameras and microphones are barred. Television cameras were not allowed in the U.S. House of Representatives until the 1970s. About half the states now let cameras in their courtrooms, but federal judges are still firm in banning cameras from their proceedings.

Semi-Public Places

After public places where cameras can roam freely, there are semi-public places – privately owned, but open to the public. Stores, restaurants, bars, offices. Anybody can walk in. There is an understood, open invitation.

The most private place is the home. Here,

criminal law says you commit a felony – not just trespass – if you enter without an invitation, even if the door is unlocked. Because of that long tradition that holds privacy of the home so sacred, most successful suits for invasion of privacy involve intrusion there.

In a truly public place, a television crew cannot invade privacy. When they walk off the sidewalk into a semi-public place, the rules shift.

Le Mistral, Inc., v. Columbia Broadcasting System, 61 A.D. 2d 491, 402 N.Y.S. 2d 815, 3 Med. L. Rptr. 1913 (1978)

Most cases now seem to indicate the camera crew can come in, camera rolling, but must leave if the owner of the semi-public place tells them to. This would apply to almost any place of business. The owner of a restaurant in New York City won a large privacy suit judgment, claiming that a television crew created a scene when they refused to leave, frightening some of his customers. Witnesses disagreed on how long the camera crew tarried, but the jury felt they overstayed their welcome.

If You Can Go There, the Camera Can, Too

Again – the camera crew has the same right of entry as the general public. The photographer has the legal right to walk into the reception area of a doctor's office, but he can't barge past the receptionist into the examining rooms, where patients have their clothes off.

In semi-public places, the outcome of a privacy suit may hinge on the behavior of the two antagonists. Juries tend to rule against people who are loud or obnoxious, and act like bullies. If a television crew enters your place of business and you ask them to leave, the nicer you are – and the pushier they are – the better your chances of winning a privacy suit. If they leave when they're asked to, they've met the privacy and trespass guidelines. The longer they refuse to leave, the more they interfere with the operation of your profession or business, the better your case.

Martin v. Struthers,
319 U.S. 141,
149 [63 S.Ct. 862,
87 L.Ed. 1313]
(1943)

Unless there is a "Do Not Enter" sign at your front gate, no trespass is committed if someone enters your property and knocks on the front door of your home. Once they knock and are asked to leave, they become trespassers if they refuse. A rented home – or a hotel room – carries with it the same sort of privacy rights as a home you own.

Electronic Eavesdropping

Most states passed laws against wiretapping in the 1920s and '30s. But they were often more concerned with the bootlegging of telephone service than with personal privacy. The proudest achievement of a well-known professional wiretapper was tapping into the Associated Press Sports Wire so his bookie client could have instant game scores and race results. The police accidentally discovered the tap, and prosecuted him.

Two- and four-party telephone service was common in most American homes through the 1940s. Most people just assumed someone might be listening to their conversations. Privacy is not a big concern if you don't expect it.

Wiretaps

A wiretap is a physical connection to a communications line – tapping into the wire that carries information. You can tap into a telephone line, a teletype line, a cable TV line and hear or see what the person at the other end of the line is receiving. One of the most vulnerable spots for industrial espionage is a telephone line that carries computerized information from one office to another.

There are no provisions in the law for private citizens to wiretap. Wiretapping is always illegal. The early laws let police agencies wiretap without supervision as part of a criminal investigation. That authority was often abused.

Bugs

During the Cold War of the 1950s, the first small "bugs" were created. Law enforcement agencies began using them on a massive scale. Each year, FBI Director J. Edgar Hoover would go before the U.S. House of Representatives committee that approved his funding, and each year he reported the number of wiretaps the FBI had used in the past 12 months – all with the approval of the U.S. Attorney General. In the years when the number of wiretaps totalled about 125, the FBI was planting hundreds – perhaps thousands – of "bugs." There was no requirement that they be reported, and very little law governing their use.

A Microphone Transmitter

A "bug" is a small combination microphone-radio transmitter. It is easy to hide, and much more intrusive than a wiretap. In a car or a room, it intercepts conversation and transmits it to a radio receiver. A "bug" can be designed to pick up not only conversation in a room, but also both ends of a telephone conversation from that room. Some of them use house current, or the voltage in the telephone line, and never need their batteries replaced. Most "bugs" have a limited range. The receiver must be located within several blocks to pick up their signal.

The invention of miniaturized electronics opened up new worlds of possibilities for privacy invasion. Their widespread use by law enforcement, as well as private investigators engaged in industrial espionage, became a major issue in the early 1960s. The law governing their use was chaos, where it existed at all. So Congress passed in 1968 — as part of its Omnibus Crime Bill — national standards for electronic eavesdropping.

Electronic Eavesdropping: The Federal Law

Simply stated, federal law says if you participate in a conversation, you may record it. But if you plant a microphone, tape recorder, or "bug" to intercept a conversation that you cannot hear, then you have committed a serious federal crime.

Under this law, police agencies must get court approval to intercept conversations if they — or their informants — are not participants. The court approval is an electronic search warrant. If a police officer goes before a judge with sworn information that you have contraband hidden in your home, the judge issues a search warrant. It gives the police the right to go into your home and search for evidence of a crime. In the same way, if a police officer has sworn information that you are about to have a conversation that would become evidence in a criminal investigation, the judge can give the officer permission to "search" that conversation with a wiretap or a "bug." The officer must certify that conventional investigative techniques will not work; that the electronic eavesdropping is a technique of last resort.

State Eavesdropping Laws

Federal law gives states power to pass more stringent eavesdropping regulations, if they choose. About half the states have made it a crime to secretly record conversations, even if you participate in that conversation. In those states, it is a felony to record your telephone calls – to record any conversation whatsoever – unless everyone whose voice is intercepted knows the microphone or "bug" is picking up what he says.

In states that have not adopted more stringent laws, you may record your telephone calls without telling the other person, if you use a suction cup or other inductance pickup that does not physically connect to the telephone company wires. You can wear a small recorder to tape conversation. In those states, television reporters can secretly record what you say and use it later in their stories.

In the more stringent states, television reporters cannot secretly record your voice, whether they use it on the air, or not.

Skirting the Law

Illinois forbids secret recording, but "60 Minutes" came up with a clever way to get around the law. They rented a storefront in Chicago and put a sign in the window announcing a doctor's office would open there soon. Representatives from about a dozen laboratories dropped in to solicit business for blood and urine tests. There was a hidden microphone, wired so the "doctor" could turn it on and off. Each time the "doctor" spoke, the mike was on. When the laboratory owners talked, the mike was off. The laboratories were offering kickbacks. Send us your business, and we'll give you a cut, under the table.

A hidden camera photographed the kickback negotiations. The audience heard the "doctor" say something like, "Now, let me get this straight – if I send you all my Medicare blood tests, you'll kick back 25 percent?"

The sound went dead, and you saw the lab man nod his head. You couldn't hear the answer, but it was easy to read his lips as he said, "That's right."

Visual Eavesdropping

So far, there are no laws establishing video privacy similar to audio privacy. If a telephoto camera lens outside can see you inside your home or business, it has not invaded your privacy. The theory seems to be — if you don't close the blinds, you can't blame your neighbors for watching you undress.

But if a secret camera were hidden inside your home or business to photograph things the reporter couldn't see with the doors and blinds closed, most judges and juries would probably feel your privacy had been invaded.

Personal Privacy

Intrusion into your personal life is another matter. It often involves some kind of physical trespass, but not necessarily.

The concept was first proposed in December, 1890 in a *Harvard Law Review* article written by two young lawyers who had roomed together in Cambridge — Samuel Warren and Louis Brandeis. Brandeis would later become one of the legendary justices of the U.S. Supreme Court. Warren's family was prominent in Boston society. They threw lavish parties. It was the heyday of Yellow Journalism. The press gossips constantly pestered the family and tried to crash their parties.

The Right To Be Left Alone

Warren and Brandeis published their novel idea in the *Harvard Law Review* essay. It is time, they said, to create a new area of law in America that would guarantee the right of personal privacy. Their definition is still used today: Personal privacy is the "right to be left alone."

Their idea took a long time to catch on. By 1950, most states still had no laws specifying personal privacy rights. Many still have none, perhaps because they are difficult to define. The lines keep changing.

In Public, You Have No Privacy

In a public place, you have almost no right of personal privacy. If the general public can see it, a television camera can shoot and broadcast what the public saw.

You may feel that a hysterical mother whose child has just been crushed by a truck has the right "to be left alone" in her grief. So far, most courts would disagree.

In the early days of television, cameras broadcasting baseball games showed people in the bleachers who were supposed to be at work. When they got into hot water with their bosses, they sued, claiming invasion of privacy. The courts held that if you are in a public place, you have no privacy protection from a camera that catches you playing hooky, or with a person who is not your spouse.

Libel and Privacy— the Differences

Let's look at the differences between libel and privacy.

Suppose you are about to be promoted to the presidency of a department store. A television reporter discovers that 40 years ago, when you were 15, you were caught shoplifting in that same store. If he broadcasts a story, there is no question that it will damage your reputation. The embarrassment could even stop your promotion. But you can't sue for libel, because it's true.

Public Good vs. Personal Privacy

You might be able to win a privacy suit. In deciding whether damages should be paid, the judicial scale tries to balance the public good that is accomplished by publishing or broadcasting information, against the damage that is done to the individual whose privacy is invaded.

Two examples:

Briscoe v. Readers Digest Assn., 4 Cal. 3d 529, 93 Cal. Rptr. 866, 483 P. 2d 34 (1971)

The *Reader's Digest,* in a long-running series on organized crime, includes a brief reference to a man who had been convicted of a crime as a young adult. The story does not focus on him. His case is simply used to illustrate a point. His wife and children, his employer, his friends knew nothing of his criminal past before the article was published. He sues for invasion of privacy, and wins. He argues he paid his debt to society, became a productive citizen, lived an exemplary life after he left prison. Any public good that was served by publicizing that part of his early life, he maintains, was far outweighed by the damage it did to his personal privacy. The court agreed.

Senator Eagleton's Past

Missouri Senator Thomas Eagleton in 1972 becomes the Democratic vice-presidential candidate, running with George McGovern. A newspaper reporter discovers that Eagleton, years earlier, had been a patient in a mental institution. The story causes Eagleton's withdrawal from the race. But there is never even a suggestion that he sue for invasion of privacy.

Why? Because he is a public official. Like libel, privacy law offers little protection to public officials.

Attitudes Change

There was a time when certain parts of public officials' lives were considered private. As a result of polio, it was extremely difficult for President Franklin D. Roosevelt to rise from a sitting position. He had to be carried in and out of automobiles. Once on his feet, with his braces locked, he could walk stiffly, slowly, with the aid of a cane. Throughout his presidency, news photographers avoided pictures that showed how handicapped he was. It was considered a matter of personal privacy.

Before John F. Kennedy was assassinated, Washington reporters began to wonder if they should report on Vice-President Lyndon Johnson's private life. Bored, alienated from Kennedy, Johnson drank a lot. He had an eye for the ladies, and frequently disappeared in the afternoons. Suppose something happened to the president, the reporters asked themselves. If there was a national emergency, would anybody know where Johnson was? And if they did, would he be able to make critical decisions?

Johnson became president, got back into working trim, and the stories were never written. The reporters were relieved. Most reporters and public officials were men, and men had a gentlemen's agreement not to talk about certain things.

The Stripper's Midnight Swim

The dam broke the night Rep. Wilbur Mills, a longtime alcoholic, got into a spat with his stripper girl friend, Fannie Fox. She jumped into the Tidal Basin and onto the front page of nearly every newspaper in the country. From that point on, nothing in a politician's private life was sacred. We were besieged with stories about the sex lives of former presidents. Since President Lyndon Johnson showed us his scar after his gall bladder operation, we expect major political figures to show us their stitches. After a fund-raising dinner, we almost demand to hear them belch.

Public People Have Less Privacy

It is not so extreme, but the same kind of attitude exists about government employees. The rule of thumb seems to be: the higher the official, and the more contact he has with the public, the less privacy. Policemen and school teachers probably have less privacy than government auditors or secretaries, on the theory that their private lives can affect the quality of their public work.

Outside government, the more visible you are, the less privacy you can expect. Officers of a major labor union or corporation expect to give up some of their privacy. Lawyers who represent famous clients or try newsworthy cases become public persons, along with entertainers and professional athletes.

We are still trying to decide just how far the media should invade private lives.

Cantrell v. Forest City Publishing Co.,
419 U.S. 245,
95 S.Ct. 465,
42 L.Ed. 2d 419
(1974)

In Ohio, a newspaper reporter and photographer return to an area that had been devastated by a flood. Their story focuses on one family. The children, at home alone, let the newsmen into the house. They tell them how the flood has changed their lives. The reporter never sees the mother. But in his story, he fudges, and includes a sentence about how tired she looks. He gives the clear impression that she was present during the interview. In deciding that the family's privacy was invaded by the story, the court makes a special note of the reporter's deception.

Privacy and Curing Cancer

In California, a *Life* magazine reporter goes to the home of a naturopathic "doctor" and feigns symptoms of cancer. The "doctor" wires the reporter to a gadget with flashing lights and tells her she is feeling bad because she ate rancid butter. He even gives her the exact day on which she ate the butter. While she is receiving his diagnosis, her "husband," a *Life* photographer, is shooting pictures with a hidden camera. He is wearing a "bug" that transmits the entire procedure to a prosecutor parked up the street in a van. When the prosecutor arrests the "doctor," *Life* magazine is there to photograph the bust. The pictures taken inside the house are featured in an article on quack doctors.

Dietemann v. Time, Inc., 449 F. 2d 245 [9th Cir.] (1971)

The naturopath sues for invasion of privacy. He wins the case, as well as the appeal. In upholding the verdict, the appellate court makes it clear that it simply does not like the idea of reporters coming into people's homes with hidden cameras and microphones, acting as agents for the police.

Barging in with the Police

A television crew is invited along on a raid at a remote school of problem children. The prosecutor obtains a search warrant, based on information that sex and drugs are part of regular activities at the school. The police barge in before dawn, pulling frightened kids out of their beds and ransacking their rooms. The camera catches everything. The officers show bags of unidentified substances, but the script leaves little doubt they found the drugs.

In the end, the police do not have a case. The television station loses a suit for privacy invasion. Here again, the facts are messy. The script is clearly written from the prosecutor's

Green Valley School, Inc., v. Cowles Florida Broadcasting, Inc., 327 So. 2d 810 (1976)

point of view. Witnesses say the officers used the television camera to intimidate people as they were being questioned. The seized pills shown in the story turn out to be tranquilizers; the apparent marijuana, herbal tea.

For generations, it has been the custom for reporters and photographers to accompany police on raids. But we may be reaching the point where that is no longer acceptable to the public. Can a television camera go along when a health inspector checks the kitchen of a restaurant? They have in the past, but attitudes are changing.

Fla. Publishing Co. v. Fletcher, 340 So. 2d 914, 2 Med. L. Rptr. 1088 [Fla. S. Ct.] (1976), cert. denied 431 U.S. 930 (1977)

A fire kills a young girl, at home alone. Her bedroom burns, and when firemen remove the body, her silhouette remains in the charred floor. A fire inspector, who does not have a camera, asks a news photographer to take a picture of the unburned spot that shows where the girl died. It is a dramatic shot, and the newspaper publishes it. The mother sues for invasion of privacy, saying the fire inspector had no right to bring the photographer into her home, and the newspaper had no right to invade her life by publishing a picture that causes her so much pain. At the trial, a jury finds the newspaper guilty of privacy invasion. On appeal, the verdict is overturned.

The lines are difficult to draw. Verdicts in one state disagree with those in another. It is new law, growing and being shaped each time a jury wrestles with the facts in a specific case.

To Recap

● If it's true, you can't win a libel suit.

● If the story is false, and you're a public official or a public person, you can win a libel suit only if you prove the television outlet had malice—that is, knew it was false, and broadcast it anyway; or they were sloppy reporters and demonstrated reckless disregard for the truth.

- True or false, a story can invade your privacy.

- You have no privacy from a camera in a public place.

- If you are in a private place, a photographer shooting with a telephoto lens from a position where he has a right to be does not invade your privacy. Broadcasting what he shoots with that telephoto lens *can* invade your privacy if a court decides your privacy outweighs any public good served by the broadcast.

- Cameramen can come into a privately owned place where the public is invited, but can become trespassers if the owner asks them to leave and they refuse.

- Federal law does not prohibit secret recording of telephone conversation by people who participate in those conversations, but about half the states have more stringent laws that prevent all secret recording by private citizens.

- Broadcasting facts about your past — and intimate portions of your present — may do more personal damage than public good, and therefore become an invasion of your privacy.

- Invasion of privacy verdicts are returned when a jury feels, "They shouldn't do that. I wouldn't like it if they did that to me."

Chapter 12

Fighting Back

When a television story is inaccurate, libelous, unfair, slanted, absurd, or just plain outrageously incompetent, what can you do about it?

In the old days, you challenged the reporter to a duel. Or thrashed him with your cane. Those techniques have gone out of style, unless you want to be the lead story in tomorrow's newspaper and perhaps make the network news.

Remember U.S. Supreme Court Chief Justice Warren Burger shoving a TV cameraman out of a hotel elevator? Guaranteed to make the news. If that's the kind of coverage you're looking for.

Most people react angrily, in ways that often create more bad stories, and worse public images for themselves. It may make you feel better – just as it would to punch the reporter – but in the end, you'll lose the fight.

Here are some of the most common reactions:

Throw Them Out

Vow never to talk to a television reporter – any television reporter – again. Hire a bouncer. Issue orders to your staff that any television photographer who sets foot on the premises is to be violently ejected.

This will endear you to all television news directors. On slow news days, it means they can count on you to liven their newscasts. "Hey, Gorilla," they'll yell across the newsroom, "Go over to Neanderthal's place and try to get in. Keep the camera rolling. We need something to fill the second block."

Great stuff. Will probably earn you a special award at the next Emmy ceremony. Best Continuing Comedy Series. Or Jackass of the Year. Marvelous for your public image.

Shut Them Out

Punish the offending station or network by shutting them out. Feed lots of stories to their competition. Hold news conferences and invite everyone else, but conveniently forget to include the offenders.

When they're unhappy with a story, this is the most common reaction in governmental agencies – particularly police departments.

It rarely works.

Most of the records reporters need for daily coverage of a public agency are – by law – public. If you shut them out, they'll go to court, and win easily. The entire process will get lots of coverage. You'll wind up with a big LOSER tag around your neck. It'll look like you're trying to hide something. The story of your shutting them out (remember Chapter Five – CONFLICT) will be a better story than those you're feeding the competition. And if they really need to know something inside your organization, their sources will leak it to them. A NO-WIN RESPONSE.

Stop the Advertising

Cancel your advertising on the offending station or network. Call your friends who advertise there and urge them to pull their commercials.

In a small town, with a small station, this may have some effect. Otherwise, you're a real candidate for Kamikaze School. Your business needs to advertise on the station a lot worse than the station needs your money. Most newscasts sell every available second of commercial time. Other companies are probably lined up, waiting to buy the time you're giving up.

145

You May Give Them New Vigor

At a station with ethical management, the advertising staff is completely divorced from the news operation. To prove that advertisers have no voice in news judgment, the news department may come after you with even more vigor than before.

If it's a station with low ratings, having a hard time selling commercials, you may hurt them a little. But losing the advertising exposure may hurt you more than it hurts them. And it'll hurt a lot more, months from now, when you come back with your hat in your hand, asking if you can place some new commercials with them.

Not a great solution. But in narrow circumstances, better than the first two.

Now, let's get down to techniques that have some hope of success.

Get to the Boss

The organizational structure at most television stations goes something like this:

The station's **general manager** hires and fires the **news director,** who is responsible for everything in the news department. The news director may have an assistant.

Each newscast has a **producer,** who's roughly the equivalent of a page editor at a newspaper. It's his job to decide which stories go into the newscast — how long they'll be, in which order, and what form.

The news director does all the hiring and firing within the news department. Reporters and photographers work under the direction of producers and the assignment editor, but their competence and any disciplinary action will be decided by the news director. Most station managers will meet with or talk to their news directors several times a day. Newscasts are the major local image-producer for a television station. If the station is a network affiliate, it has no control or responsibility for the network programming it broadcasts.

News directors and station managers are human, too. Their natural reaction will be to defend their employees, and their stories.

It's Important To Complain

But it's important to complain when you feel strongly that a reporter or a station has broadcast an incompetent, or unfair, or dishonest story. The first time he receives a complaint, the news director may not have any discernible reaction. But if he receives a second or third complaint about the same reporter or photographer, he will begin to wonder whether he has a problem on his staff who could get him – and the station – into much more serious trouble.

Make Your Own Tape

The FCC does not require broadcasters to keep a copy of their scripts or a tape of their broadcasts. They are not required to provide you with a copy of what they said. If you have any advance warning that a story may be slanted or antagonistic, you should at least make an audio recording of the broadcast. A videotape recording is much better.

Complaining:

These are the steps to take if you have a complaint about a story:

Step 1

Call the reporter. Discuss it with him. If you feel a correction is called for, ask for it. If you're unhappy with his response, take the next step.

Step 2   **Write the news director** a detailed letter describing your complaint with the story or his staff member's behavior. Quote from the offensive story and write, in detail, your version of what happened; or how the story is inaccurate or unfair. Send a copy of the letter to the station manager. If you're still unhappy, go to Step 3.

Step 3   **Write the station manager** the same kind of detailed letter. This time, send a copy to the president of the corporation that owns the station. You can usually get the names and addresses by calling the station manager's secretary. If not, go to the station and ask to see the PUBLIC FILE. This is a file required by the FCC which will include fairly complete details of station ownership and corporate officers; and what the station committed to do when it applied for its license with the FCC. If your complaint involves fairness or deception, or something that might lead to a lawsuit, send a copy of this letter to the corporate vice-president for legal affairs.

Step 4   **Now it's time to write the president** of the corporation.

Local television stations are usually much more responsive to complaints than newspapers. They're always concerned about their public image. Anything that turns off viewers lowers their ratings. What they can charge for advertising time is directly related to how many people are watching.

TV Is Sensitive   Many station managers require their telephone switchboard operators to keep a daily log of calls – both complaints and praise. It gives them a daily survey of audience reaction to their programming. The FCC also requires voluminous "ascertainment interviews." These are personal interviews with all segments of the community. At license renewal time, the station is supposed to show how its programming has served the community's needs, as reflected in those interviews.

If you're contemplating a lawsuit against the station, you should consider having your lawyer look at each of your letters before you send them. He might want to send them as your attorney, or send a cover letter along with yours.

Tell the Newspaper

Competing local media may be interested in reporting a television station's goof or breach of journalistic ethics — especially print media.

Regional magazines often cover local television better than the newspaper. Since they don't compete daily, it's okay for them to acknowledge readers' interest in television news.

This idea of the media tattling on each other is fairly new. In some cities, they still refuse to report each other's indiscretions. After all, the next embarrassing story could be about me, if this thing gets out of hand.

Write a letter to the editor of the local newspaper. If the newspaper has a television critic, give him a call. Newspaper Sunday supplements and regional magazines are often interested in semi-investigative stories that expose shoddy television reporting or policy.

Tell the Competition

A few television stations have media critics that are always looking for material. They'd love to hear from you if there's a story of sloppy, inaccurate reporting or slanted, unfair treatment. In some cities, public television stations have regular reviews of local reporting.

In 1983, *TV Guide* wrote a scorching story about a CBS documentary that had suggested General William Westmoreland conspired to hide or distort reports on enemy strength and casualties in Vietnam. Hodding Carter, former press secretary for the State Department, also did an investigative special for Public Broadcasting on the same CBS documentary.

ABC was a pioneer with periodic programs that examined some of its own news coverage. After Geraldo Rivera did a piece for "20/20" claiming that aluminum wiring was a serious fire hazard in thousands of American homes, a spokesman for the industry had a chance to sit across from Rivera in the studio and debate the accuracy of that story, with Ted Koppel as referee.

Complaining to a Network

Effectively complaining about a network news story is much more difficult. The networks have regional bureaus across the country. Correspondents work out of those bureaus. They spend about four days a week on the road. If you're interviewed by a network correspondent, chances are you'll never see him again. His immediate supervisor will be a bureau chief hundreds of miles away. The people with the real power are in New York.

Know the Bureau and Producer

If you're interviewed by a network correspondent, find out which bureau he's assigned to, and the name of the field producer for the story. A network crew will usually include the correspondent, a field producer, photographer and sound technician. The correspondent is the one you'll see and hear when the story is broadcast. The producer does most of the work. The field producer scouts the story, sets up interviews, gathers documents, manages travel arrangements, figures a way to hustle the videotape to New York by plane or satellite, and may even write the script the correspondent reads.

If you try to call a network bureau to complain to the correspondent or producer, they probably won't be there. They're running to catch a plane halfway around the world. So start working your way up the hierarchy.

1. **Phone the bureau chief.** Give him your opinion of the story and its failings. During the conversation, ask who his immediate supervisor is. Each network is organized differently.

2. **Write his superior.** At each stage, send a copy of your letter to the next one up the ladder.

3. **Write the head of network news.** The title of the news division boss varies from time to time. He may be president of XYZ News, which is a division of the XYZ Network. Or the network may have several vice-presidents — one of them in charge of news. Remember to be detailed and specific with your complaint. And if you're still not happy with the response:

4. **Write the president of the network.** If there's any thought of a lawsuit, send a copy to the vice-president for legal affairs. You can get the names and addresses of network executives by calling ABC, CBS or NBC in New York.

Complaining to the FCC

The Federal Communications Commission processes about 175,000 complaints every year. Most of the people who write get back a form letter asking for more detailed information. Here — more so than with a complaint to a station or network — great detail is extremely important if you expect to have any impact. The local station or network knows exactly which story you're talking about, and precisely what they said. The FCC has no way of knowing.

You Must Give Details

So you have to give them the station or network that broadcast the story, the date, which newscast, the correspondent or anchorperson who read it, quotes from the story (a transcript of exactly what was said will impress them) and why the story is inaccurate, unfair or deceptive.

Send your complaint to:

Federal Communications Commission
Mass Media Bureau
Enforcement Division
1919 M Street NW
Washington, D.C. 20554

The revocation of a broadcast license is extremely rare. Virtually every revocation in the history of the FCC was based on some kind of deception. But the loss of its license is so threatening, a station always sits up and takes notice if the FCC begins an inquiry.

An FCC Experiment

In 1982, the FCC began an experimental program in five southeastern states. Complaints from viewers in Florida, Georgia, South Carolina, Tennessee and Louisiana will be forwarded to the broadcasters' associations in those states. The associations will determine whether the complaints are valid and try to mediate the disputes. If the complainant is not satisfied with the results, the state association will send the case back to the FCC, with suggestions. This is an effort to have complaints investigated by a local agency which has more knowledge of both the station and the story. On the other hand, the station that is the target of the complaint is also a member of the group that will be doing the investigating. It's still too early to tell whether the experiment will work.

The National News Council

In the entire history of the United States, government has never used its power to intimidate and harass the news media as energetically as it did during the Nixon Administration. Until he was charged with a federal crime and forced to resign, Nixon's vice-president, Spiro Agnew, was the administration's hatchet man for the press. It was Charles Colson's job at the White House to watch all three network newscasts each evening. If he saw something about the administration he didn't like, he called the network in New York and demanded to talk to the anchorperson immediately, while the newscast was in progress. Occasionally, he succeeded, during a commercial break. It was an effective way to badger the network.

What Checks and Balances the Media?

Agnew kept suggesting that the news media had become too powerful. That some agency ought to be created to control them. How that could be done without repealing the First Amendment was never explained. But a lot of people agreed with him.

In that atmosphere, the National News

Council was born, as a privately financed group to investigate complaints about the news media. For some, it was an idea whose time had come. Others, hoped a private review of complaints would slow the campaign to create some kind of governmental control for the press.

Only the Power To Embarrass

The council has no power, except the power to embarrass news organizations that are dishonest, inaccurate or unfair. It receives about 750 complaints every year. A staff of five culls out the trivia. In the past, about 13 percent of the complaints were considered serious enough to open a case file. Investigators interview the complainants, gather documents, go to the newspaper or television outlet and get its side of the story.

Open-and-shut cases are handled entirely by staff. The more complex situations—particularly ethics and conflicts of interest questions—often get a full hearing by the council's prestigious board of directors. The board holds a full hearing and files its conclusions in about 25 cases every year.

The council gets half its financing from foundations; one-quarter from the media, and one-quarter from individuals and corporate contributors.

But Few People See the Slap

The council's major drawback has been the limited circulation of its findings. A slap from the council is embarrassing within the profession, but few non-professionals ever hear about it. The Associated Press and United Press International carry short stories when the council criticizes a newspaper or television station. The target of the criticism may carry the wire story on an inside page, where it doesn't get much attention.

The exception is the *New York Times,* which doesn't carry the story at all. It has always opposed, on principle, the idea of the National News Council.

CBS News has a written policy *requiring* a story if the council criticizes CBS.

Until 1982, the full text of council reports was printed in the *Columbia (University) Journalism Review.* They're now printed in *Quill* – a journalistic society magazine with limited circulation. The council is trying now to build more rapport with newspaper ombudsmen, hoping they'll be inclined to give more coverage to the council's investigations.

In the past, few complaints have been filed with the council about local television stories. Perhaps because so few people know the council is there.

If you have a complaint that has major significance for the news media, write:

**The National News Council
One Lincoln Plaza
New York, N.Y. 10023**

Groups with Special Concerns

There are a number of other national organizations designed to fight for specific causes and television's coverage of those causes. Some lobby for what they believe would be better television. Things like less violence, less sexuality, more programming of one kind or another. Some of these organizations have money and staff to help you carry a complaint to court, to Congress or the FCC. Most of them, however, will be interested in your complaint only if it fits their narrow area of interest.

The Columbia Journalism Review

The *Columbia Journalism Review,* founded in 1961, has become the conscience of television news. In its first edition, it defined its purpose:

> *"To assess the performance of journalism in all its forms, to call attention to its shortcomings and strengths, and to help define — or redefine — standards of honest, responsible service... to help stimulate continuing improvement in the profession and to speak out for what is right, fair, and decent."*

Each year, the *Review* publishes a survey of broadcast journalism, trying to show new trends, both good and bad. The duPont-Columbia Award is broadcasting's most prestigious prize; the equivalent of the Pulitzer Prize for print journalism.

Bi-Monthly Darts and Laurels

The *Review* is published bi-monthly by the Graduate School of Journalism at Columbia University. In each issue, there is a section called "Darts and Laurels," in which the staff praises or roasts networks, local stations, and the print media, giving details on each story that deserves a dart or a laurel. The editors are always interested in a major story, or a pattern of performance and policy that violate journalistic ethics. If it's serious enough, they'll assign a reporter to investigate and publish a full story in the magazine.

Criticism in the *Columbia Journalism Review* is probably the most widely circulated embarrassment in the news business.

If you think the editors would be interested in your complaint, write:

The Columbia Journalism Review
700 Journalism Building
Columbia University
New York, N.Y. 10027

Sigma Delta Chi and Quill

Sigma Delta Chi is a national honorary journalism society, which has created a code of ethics for journalists. Most major cities have a local Sigma Delta Chi chapter. Call the city desk at the local newspaper to find the name of the Sigma Delta Chi president in your city. Give him a call and tell him about your complaint. The initiative and strength of the organization varies a lot from city to city. A strong chapter, incensed over a story that was inaccurate, unfair or unethical, might pass a resolution condemning the offending television station.

Quill is Sigma Delta Chi's national magazine. It now publishes the National News Council's reports. (They were originally published by the *Columbia Journalism Review*.) *Quill* also publishes articles that criticize journalistic performance, but its circulation and influence are smaller than the *Columbia Journalism Review*.

You can write the editor at:

The Quill
840 N. Lake Shore Dr.
Suite 801W
Chicago, IL 60611

Local Journalism Reviews

Some cities have local journalism reviews, often written and distributed free among local journalists. In some cases, they are almost underground publications, where local reporters write anonymously about scandals inside their

station or publication. Again, ask the newspaper city desk if it is aware of any local journalism review and how to get in touch with
its editor.

Area Schools of Communications

A school of journalism or communications
in your area probably has personal contact
with some of the people in local television
news. The news director may be one of its
graduates.

While a journalism school usually has no
formal way to investigate or criticize poor
journalistic performance, the dean might be
able to quietly shake his finger and influence
the station the next time a similar situation
occurs.

Chapter 13

Off the Record and Other Games

You can no longer be sure what "off the record" means. The Washington press corps has created half a dozen gradations for talking to the news media in confidence. They accept information for "background only." Or "deep background." Or quotes for "non-attribution." Few people outside the Washington bureaucracy know what they're talking about. And even insiders are sometimes confused.

Before you tell something to a reporter in confidence, be sure you both understand the terms on which you give – and he receives– the information. There should be a clear verbal contract before you stick your neck out. That contract is terribly important. If it's broken, you could lose your job, your reputation, or your life. He could lose his career. Or wind up in jail.

The Contract Comes First

Talking to a reporter, and then adding, "Now, that's off the record" won't work. The contract must be made *before* the information is given. You can't spill the beans in front of him and then ask him not to tell.

Most good reporters won't accept information if they have to pledge they'll never use it. Their job is to gather and broadcast information, not store it in their heads. They may already know what you're about to tell them. Promising you they will never tell would prevent them from using it.

Your approach to a reporter should be, "I'd like to tell you something in confidence." If the reporter is not experienced enough to explore exactly what you mean, you should spell it out for him. Variations of the contract:

1. **The reporter may use the information**

in any way he chooses, so long as he is very careful not to quote you directly, or to even hint where it came from. This kind of information is often attributed to a "confidential source" or a "highly reliable source."

2. **The reporter can indicate the organization or group you represent.** The story's credibility is increased if the source is less vague. "A confidential source in the police department." Or "a highly-placed executive in a major oil company." This part of the contract may be especially critical. Confidential sources often ignore it, leaving it to the reporter to disguise the source. The problem here is that the reporter can unintentionally identify you to insiders. "A veteran executive in the power company's research and planning division" may tell everybody in the company you are the source, since nobody else has been there more than two years. Your leak will be a lot safer if you discuss with the reporter the exact words he will use in referring to his source.

3. **You may want the reporter to hold the story until a later time.** "I want you to be aware of this," you tell him, "because I know you'll need some advance work to write a better story when it breaks." Lengthy police investigations are often leaked in advance to the press on this basis. Television, in particular, needs extra time to look for file tape, to collect pictures of people, to shoot "real estate" (buildings or places where parts of the story took place), to produce charts or diagrams that will help explain complicated figures or relationships.

If the information is leaked for later use, be

sure to discuss with the reporter how covert he must be in gathering background material to avoid tipping your hand. Stories like the retirement or appointment of a key executive; the introduction of a new model or product; the filing of a lawsuit; a revolutionary medical technique.

There is always a risk to the reporter if he accepts information and agrees to hold it until later. His competition may find out about it, and beat him to the story. Some contracts provide for that. The reporter agrees to hold what you've told him until the agreed time *unless his competitors are about to break the story.* If that is imminent, then he may go with it. This will involve your being able to trust him when he tells you tomorrow he has to go with the story or be beaten. You also have an obligation to tip him if one of his competitors approaches you, asking questions about the story.

4. **"You may use this information if you can confirm it with another source."** This, also, involves trust on your part. It is usually used if you're afraid so few people know about it, the story would immediately point the finger at you. The information may be more widespread than you realize. If the reporter can find it somewhere else, you will not be as suspect.

5. **Backgrounding.** "I want you to be aware of some things that are happening. In the next few days or weeks, a story will break, and then you'll understand the importance of what I'm about to tell you. You must not do anything that would ever suggest you received this briefing from me."

6. **No quotes.** "You may use everything I'm about to tell you, and use my name, so long as you don't quote me directly. You must paraphrase what I say." This is a protection for the source, in case there is bad public reaction to a trial balloon. You can always come back with, "Let me clarify my position on this."

7. **"You may never attribute anything to me unless I specifically say, 'You can quote me.'"** This is a time-saving device if you have a continuing confidential source relationship with a reporter. You understand that there is a continuing contract that is in operation every time you talk, unless you make an exception.

Other Conditions

There are other conditions that should be clear when you make your contract with a reporter:

Does the reporter have authority to promise you confidence? In some news organizations, only a supervisor can give that pledge.

Will Others Know?

Will others in the news operation be aware of your identity? When Janet Cooke wrote her fictitious story about a child heroin addict, she did not tell her editors at the *Washington Post* how she found the boy, or where he lived. She said she was doing it to protect the confidential agreement that led her to the boy. She won the Pulitzer Prize before the story was unmasked as fiction. Embarrassed, the newspaper had to admit the hoax and return the prize. Because of that danger, many stations require supervisors or station attorneys to know the identity of sources for some stories that hinge on confidential information.

Would You Go to Jail?

You should ask how far the reporter is willing to go to protect your confidence. Would he go to jail rather than disclose you as his source?

If giving a reporter information in confidence poses any kind of threat to you, you should know a lot about the reporter and the company he works for. It is a matter of character judgment and trust on your part.

Shield Laws

Some states have shield laws that give reporters legal protection for confidential information. They cannot be forced to disclose their confidential sources. Most states shield ministers, lawyers and accountants from being forced to disclose information given them in confidence. There was an assumption that reporters had that same kind of shield under the First Amendment until the 1970s, when the U.S. Supreme Court ruled otherwise. If a state wants to give reporters that protection, it may, the Supreme Court said. But if the state does not, then a judge may decide whether the public good is more important than the reporter's claim of First Amendment rights. The judge can order the reporter to disclose his source. And if he refuses, the reporter can be held in contempt of court and jailed until he obeys the court order.

Confidential Sources and Libel

Confidential sources raise major problems if the reporter and his company are sued for libel. To win a libel suit, they must prove the story is true (or, in the case of a public person, that they broadcast the story, believing it was true). If it is based on confidential sources, they have no way to prove truth. In some states, their refusal to answer questions during the pre-trial discovery process will result in an automatic judgment against them. The only question then for the jury is how much in damages to award the libel victim.

An Affidavit with an Escape Clause

One way to cover that possibility is to give the reporter a sworn affidavit, with a written agreement that your identity will be kept confidential *unless* it is needed to defend a lawsuit. If that happens, you agree that the reporter can disclose your identity, and the contents of your sworn statement. This technique is invaluable if the story is extremely sensitive.

Several years ago, a group of doctors at a major hospital became concerned about several staff members. A heart specialist was performing experimental, unnecessary surgery on elderly patients so he could publish his findings in medical journals. The death rate in those operations was very high. Anesthesiologists at the same hospital were not even present during major surgery. They substituted interns, but the patient was billed as though the more experienced anesthesiologist had been there.

A number of more ethical doctors on the staff became concerned, but were reluctant to go public with their accusations. They leaked internal hospital records to a television reporter, and gave her sworn affidavits about what they had seen and heard in the hospital. On the back of each affidavit, the reporter gave the doctors a written agreement never to disclose the doctor's identity unless his statement was needed to defend a lawsuit.

In her script, the reporter said, "I have sworn affidavits from a dozen doctors who say they have seen..." There was never even a suggestion of a lawsuit from either the doctors or the hospital. They knew the reporter had the evidence that could convince a jury the story was true.

In a Plain Brown Wrapper

An anonymous telephone call to a reporter is sometimes all it takes to get the story out. Or copies of documents, mailed to the reporter in a plain envelope. The reporter is protected in that way, too. If his source ever becomes the focus of a grand jury investigation, he can honestly say, "I don't know who sent those papers to me."

Another technique for leaking information is to write a detailed internal memo and circulate it widely. If a copy winds up in a reporter's hands, or his mailbox, it could have been leaked by lots of people.

Out-Takes

There are a number of ethical guidelines in the news media that often puzzle outsiders. None is more baffling than the refusal to give up out-takes. Out-takes are film or videotape that were shot, but never published or broadcast. In the editing process, they were taken out. Editors decided to use other pictures.

Chicago in 1968

The out-take issue took on national significance in the summer of 1968, after the street demonstrations during the Democratic National Convention in Chicago. Those demonstrations were some of the first major protests, involving thousands of people, against the Vietnam War. Both federal and state prosecutors decided it was time to treat protestors more harshly. They went to newspapers and television stations with subpoenas, demanding all film and still pictures taken during the demonstrations. From those pictures, they planned to prosecute anyone they could identify.

Many editors and news directors had never dealt with the issue before. Some handed over their out-takes. Others refused, saying they would destroy the pictures and risk contempt of court.

Many people could not understand why they thought themselves immune to subpoenas and court orders. The police were using pictures already printed and broadcast to round up protestors. What was the difference between those and out-takes?

Out-Takes and the First Amendment

The argument against giving up out-takes uses a First Amendment theory. "If I give you these pictures," the news media argue, "and you use them to prosecute people, then my photographers have become police agents. The public will know that. At the next demonstration, the crowd will attack the photographers to prevent their getting evidence for the police. We will not be able to cover the demonstration, because we will be perceived as policemen. Therefore, the government subpoena violates the First Amendment. Congress (government) shall make no law (order) abridging freedom of the press."

We Won't Give Up Our Out-Takes

After the 1968 hassle, many news organizations adopted a broad policy that says, "We will never give up out-takes to any governmental agency. We will destroy the pictures or hide them and risk contempt of court rather than handicap ourselves in future news gathering."

Other news organizations take a case-by-case approach. "In some instances," they say, "we can give up out-takes without jeopardizing future freedom to gather news."

Their critics say, "If you do it once, you set up a precedent that will make it harder to refuse out-takes next time."

It is a tough question.

Suppose, for instance, that a television reporter is shooting a standup in a downtown park. He flubs several times. The sun goes in and out behind the clouds. The photographer is unhappy with the light, so he asks the reporter to do it once more. An airplane passes over and the sound is ruined, so they do it again. They use one of the standups in a story for the six o'clock news. The six flawed standups become out-takes.

Well, Almost Never

The next morning, a police detective shows up at the newsroom. "I understand you were shooting videotape in Downtown Park yesterday about two o'clock," he says. "I'd like to look at that tape. There was an armed robbery in a jewelry store across the street from the park at 2:05. A clerk, in the store alone, was killed. Your camera may have photographed the killer as he entered or left the store. Right now, we have no other leads."

Is there now a reasonable argument to deny the police access to the out-takes? Some organizations will give them up in a narrow circumstance like this. There is a loophole for the station with the "no out-takes" policy. They could look at the videotape, and if it does show someone going in or out of the jewelry store, they could run it on the news tonight. Great follow-up to the murder story. Once on the air, it would no longer be an out-take, and the station could honor a subpoena without violating its policy.

Reporters as Police Agents

Twenty-five years ago, there was little concern about reporters becoming police agents. Policemen and reporters often collaborated. The police gave reporters story leads, and the reporters passed information to the police. A two-way street. It is still common in cities like Chicago for reporters to pursue an investigative story until they reach a dead-end, then turn it over to a prosecutor who can use the police and his subpoena power to get information the reporter can't reach. They agree that if the information makes a criminal case, the reporter who supplied it gets an exclusive when it's time to make arrests.

Some people in the news business are beginning to question that kind of coziness between the media and the police. It is not the media's job to make criminal cases, they say. That is a function of the criminal justice system. To become a police informant, they say, compromises a reporter's independence; there should be a more arm's-length relationship between reporters and the governmental agencies they cover.

In some organizations, one reporter is assigned the police beat. He becomes a closet cop. Reporters who might be assigned to investigate police misconduct or corruption are careful not to do any favors—or accept any—from the police.

Should Reporters Be Witnesses?

Some news organizations have severe misgivings about their employees testifying in a criminal trial, or before a grand jury. In the early 1970s, three reporters in separate incidents refused to even go inside grand jury rooms. They had been subpoenaed to testify about illegal activities they had witnessed and written about. They said they arranged to watch those activities by promising that they would never disclose the names of the people involved. If they went into a secret grand jury session, they argued, and their sources were later arrested, the sources would believe the reporters had talked inside the grand jury room.

The U.S. Supreme Court combined the three incidents because they were so similar, and in one decision ruled that reporters have no First Amendment immunity from grand jury subpoenas. The Court said a reporter might refuse to testify about certain things once he gets in the witness chair, and that refusal might have to be argued in court; but there are many other subjects a reporter is obligated to talk about, just as any other citizen.

Junkets and Freebies

A hundred years ago, P.T. Barnum — or one of his protégés — learned how to get free advertising when the circus came to town. First, you hired schoolboys to paste circus posters on the side of every barn within 20 miles. They'd do it for nothing if you gave them free circus tickets. Newspaper reporters were the same way. All it took was a batch of free tickets, and a reporter would write a glowing story about that wondrous extravaganza of excitement, that colossal collection of color and courage, that stunning display of spine-tingling skill waiting for you under the Big Top.

It still works.

Until the early 1970s, it was not unusual for reporters to accept all sorts of freebies. Travel writers took elaborate trips, with an airline or a resort picking up the tab. Political writers traveled with a candidate in planes the candidate or the party paid for. Press rooms were provided in public buildings for free. Critics received free tickets to the events they reviewed, and sportswriters almost universally accepted batches of season tickets for every conceivable event that was related in any way to sports within a hundred miles.

An investigative story in a magazine caused a major furor. It told how sportswriters at major newspapers accepted large numbers of valuable season tickets, which they could sell or pass out to ingratiate themselves with other people. Embarrassed newspapers began announcing they would no longer accept free tickets to sports or cultural events. Many news organizations drew up—some for the first time—a code of ethics for their staffs. Most now forbid accepting gifts or anything of value from any person or organization a reporter might expect to cover. Some are so strict, they won't even let their employees accept a free lunch. They pay their pro rata share of transportation costs when they travel with candidates, and they even pay rent for the use of press rooms in public buildings.

All of those policies are evolving as news organizations become more sensitive to their own conflicts of interest. If they constantly search for conflicts of interest among public officials and corporate executives, they have to keep their own skirts clean.

Checkbooks and Journalism

Checkbook journalism became a nasty term in the middle 1970s after CBS paid H.R. Haldeman $25,000 for a lengthy interview. Haldeman had been Richard Nixon's White House chief of staff. Throughout the Watergate investigation, Haldeman had said nothing to the news media. The CBS interview was a coup that backfired.

Paying an interviewee raises the same questions that come up when a paid informer testifies at a criminal trial. Can you really believe someone who's been paid to talk? Was he paid to say that? Was there an agreement to avoid certain subjects? Would he have talked about them if the price had been high enough?

Because the Haldeman interview received so much adverse publicity, it would be extremely rare today for a television news organization to pay someone for an interview. But newspapers and magazines still pay people for "exclusivity." *Life* magazine signed a lucrative contract with the original group of astronauts for their exclusive, personal stories, and nothing much was said about it.

The concept of what you can pay for, without tainting the story, is still evolving.

Reviewing Scripts

Interviewees often ask if they can see a script before the story goes on the air. That's considered a no-no. If you saw it, and didn't like what the reporter wrote, or the way he presented the story, you'd tell him. And that might influence him to change it. He would lose his independence. In effect, you would become an editor for a story about yourself. So don't ask.

Air Everything I Say or Nothing

If you're doing battle with a television news organization, you may not trust their editing of what you say on-camera. Many people in this situation say they'll submit to an on-camera interview only if the station agrees to broadcast it, unedited.

This kind of offer is almost always refused. As a part of their FCC licensing, broadcasters accept responsibility for everything they put on the air. In effect, they would be handing that responsibility to someone else. They can be sued if you use their station to libel someone. You might be irresponsible in other ways, like using four-letter words the FCC frowns on.

There's a way around the problem. Draw up a letter of agreement in which the station says it will broadcast everything you say in an on-camera statement or interview – or nothing at all. That leaves them complete editorial control of what goes on their air.

It Must Be Brief

If you expect them to use what you say under that agreement, remember – it has to be brief, and to the point.

In Closing...

Well, now you have the basics.
The more you understand about TV news the more your terror will ease the next time a camera is poked in your face or your office. If you can learn to be yourself, to let us see you without the shields up; if you can tell us what you really think and feel in 50 words or less, you've got it made.

It takes practice, and mental discipline. But if you expect to succeed in business or politics, within your profession or any project where you have to reach the public, it's a language you must learn.

Invest in a VCR

If you expect to be on television from time to time, a home videocassette recorder is a good investment. Tape news and interview shows so you can study their formats and style, especially those where you might appear. When you do, make sure your segment is video-taped so you can examine your own performance. Have someone else look at it and give you an honest evaluation. Most of us have a hard time seeing ourselves as others see us, even on videotape.

Go to School

If you're really unhappy with the way you look or talk on camera, there are a number of schools around the country that offer intensive weekend seminars to improve your skills. Professors at journalism schools sometimes moonlight by giving individual tutoring.

Buy a Camera

Speech teachers used to recommend rehearsing your speech in front of a mirror. Don't rehearse for television. But if you're really serious about improving your television technique, you might buy or rent a video camera

that will plug into your videocassette recorder.
Invite a friend over, get the camera rolling,
and videotape your conversation. Talk about
serious things, and tell funny stories, until you
truly think of the camera as another person
in the living room, listening and taking part.

Now You Know How To Speak TV

When that happens, and you can organize
your conversation in concise building blocks,
you'll discover that you've become fluent in
another language. That you've learned to
speak TV.

Glossary of TV Terms

Ambush Interview A sudden confrontation with a TV news crew, in which the interview subject is ambushed, caught by surprise, and frequently appears guilty or furtive. See Chapter 9.

Anchor The person who introduces news stories, usually in the TV studio, during a newscast. The anchor will also read stories alone where a reporter is not seen or heard. The job gets its name from a ship anchor, which is supposed to hold the ship firm, no matter which way the wind blows. In TV news, most formats revolve around the anchor or anchor team, as the focal point giving the newscast its style and direction, moving it from one story to another. For anchor story formulas, see Chapter 1.

Assignment Editor The person in a newsroom who decides each day how the station's reporters and photographers will be used. Expected to know what is happening, and dispatch the station's resources to best cover them. One of the most hectic jobs in television news. The person to notify when you think you have a story for TV. See Chapter 7.

Audio The sound you hear during a TV newscast, as distinguished from video – what you see. During the editing process, audio and video are sometimes inserted separately into the videocassette that will eventually be broadcast as a reporter's story. See Chapter 4.

Bite Short for sound bite. A small portion of a videotaped interview which is edited into the reporter's story. Usually less than 20 seconds. In network news stories, frequently less than 10 seconds. One bite is sometimes edited to another in a way that makes it appear both sentences or phrases were spoken together, in sequence. See Chapter 4.

Bug A very small radio transmitter, used to secretly broadcast conversation to a receiver, usually several blocks away. Illegal under FCC rules and regulations, except for police. A felony under federal law if nobody in that intercepted conversation is aware of the electronic eavesdropping. In some states, illegal under state law even if one party to the conversation is aware. See Chapter 11.

Chroma-Key An electronic device used by a TV station to insert graphics or video in the broadcast picture. Often used to insert a generic graphic over the shoulder of the anchor.

Control Room The nerve center of the television station, where a director, sitting at a huge board of lights, switches and TV monitors, controls what goes out over the air. The buttons and switches in the control room start and stop machines in other parts of the station – cameras, microphones, videotape players, film projectors, etc. See Chapter 1.

Copy Story A news story read by the anchor in which there is no reporter and no videotape. Sometimes called a "reader." See Chapter 1.

Correspondent The proper title for network reporters, probably because they are always on the road. They were given this title in the early days of TV news, in the same way that newspapers have traditionally called their out-of-town reporters correspondents.

Cutaway An editing shot, used to cover an edit point, or "jump cut." The most frequently used cutaways show the reporter listening or taking notes; the crowd during a meeting or a speech; or a "two-shot," in which we see both the reporter and the interview subject from a great distance – far enough away that we cannot tell whether the movement of the interview subject's lips matches the words we're hearing. See Chapter 4.

Dissolve The fading out of one picture while another fades in. Frequently used to make the transition from one place to another less jarring.

Dub A videotape copy. The sound and picture are dubbed from one videocassette onto another.

ENG Shorthand for electronic news gathering – the revolution in technology which took place in the 1970s, when most networks and local stations switched from film to videotape.

Equal Time A requirement by the FCC and federal law that any broadcast licensee who gives time to a political candidate during the election process must give equal time to his opponent. Only politicians get equal time. See Chapter 10.

Fairness Doctrine An FCC requirement that broadcast licensees must present all sides of controversial issues of public importance. Not to be confused with Equal Time. See Chapter 10.

FCC The Federal Communications Commission, appointed by the president and confirmed by the Senate, to regulate broadcasting in the United States. See Chapters 10 and 12.

Field Interview An interview videotaped in the field – away from a television studio.

Field Producer A producer assigned to work with a reporter or TV camera crew in the field, as distinguished from a producer who acts as editor and production manager for a specific newscast.

Freeze Frame   A single frame of video, taken from a moving videotaped picture. Sometimes used when the picture is so fleeting most viewers will not get a chance to see what the camera recorded. In effect, a still picture taken from movie film or videotape.

Graphic   A picture, drawn by an artist, or a graph used to help illustrate a TV story. Graphics are often used when there is no videotape to cover a section of the reporter's script. Sometimes used to distinguish between a still picture or drawing and video that has movement and sound.

Grip   Another name for the camera assistant who works with a TV news photographer. Grips will usually double as sound technicians, monitoring the quality and level of sound picked up by the mike and recorded on videotape.

Hot   TV term for sound that is too loud or light that is too bright.

In-Cue   The first words of a sound bite. Sometimes written into the script to help an editor find the bite the reporter wants edited into the story at that point. See Chapter 4.

Jump Cut   The point at which an interview is edited, where a second phrase or sentence is spliced to the first. Gets it name because the interview subject appears to suddenly jump where the videotape was edited. (With videotape, unlike film, cutting and splicing are done electronically. The original version of the interview remains intact. The edited version is a dub on a second cassette.) Jump cuts are usually covered by a cutaway shot for esthetic reasons. TV news has not yet agreed on a system like the print journalist's ellipsis, which would tell viewers an edit was made. See Chapter 4.

Key   Short for Chroma-Key. The picture inserted, or "keyed" into a small section of the television screen.

Lead-in   The introduction to a TV news story read by the anchor. Usually less than 15 seconds. A headline, designed to tell you what the story is about and alert you to pay attention.

Live Shot   A reporter standup or interview relayed back to the TV station for immediate, live broadcast during a newscast.

Market   The area served by a television station. Usually about 30 or 40 miles in all directions.

Microwave   The radio frequency used to transmit audio and video back to a television station for re-broadcast. Live shots are microwaved to the station, then converted to the broadcast band for immediate, live transmission.

Mixer   An electronic device which allows a videotape editor to mix two sounds and edit them onto a videocassette. The reporter's voice is some-times mixed with natural sound from the videotape that he is describing, or which covers his narration.

Natural Sound   Sometimes called "wild sound." The back-ground noise that is present everywhere except in an acoustically padded booth. A reporter will sometimes use natural sound, full volume, to let you hear the noise of a gun battle, the crackle of a fire, the collapse of a building that was recorded on videotape. Natural sound is usually mixed with the reporter's voice when he is narrating, voice-over, video-tape. See Chapter 4.

Network A network to broadcast TV programs nationwide. Local stations affiliated with a network
agree to broadcast locally the network's programming, but are not owned or controlled by
that network. Each major network owns five
VHF stations, the maximum allowed under
FCC regulations. See Chapter 6.

News Director The person in charge of everything in a local
TV station's news department. The person
who hires and fires reporters, anchors and
photographers. See Chapter 12.

O and O One of the local stations owned and operated
by a network. See Chapter 6.

Out-Cue The last phrase in a sound bite. Sometimes
written into the script, along with the in-cue,
to help an editor find the bite the reporter
wants edited into the story at that point. See
Chapter 4.

Out-Takes Film or videotape shot by a TV news crew
which is not broadcast. Often the center of
conflict between government and TV news
operations. Some organizations, as a matter of
principle, refuse to give up out-takes, even if
they are subpoenaed. See Chapter 13.

Package The term used at some stations for a reporter's
story, complete within itself, "packaged" on
a videocassette. Sometimes called a "wrap" or
a "Sony Sandwich." See Chapter 2.

Peanut TV term for a small microphone, about the size
of a peanut, that clips to your tie or collar.

PIO Short for Public Information Officer. The person designated by governmental agencies or
private business to act as spokesman and to
help reporters find people and information
within the organization. See Chapter 7.

Pot   A technical term for a volume control. Sound is "potted up" or "potted down."

Producer   The person who decides how a TV newscast will be organized; the order of the stories; how long they will be, and how they will be produced. Roughly the equivalent of a page editor or section editor at a newspaper. See Field Producer.

Public File   A public record required by the FCC to be available at each broadcast licensee's office, giving corporate or ownership information about the station, its application for licensing, and certain publications explaining how the FCC regulates broadcasters. See Chapter 12.

Rating   The percentage of households in a market area who own a television set who are watching a certain program or station at any given time. A rating point is one percent of the entire potential audience watching a given show. See Share and Chapter 6.

Reader   A story read by an anchor without visuals or reporter involvement. Also called a "copy story." See Chapter 1.

Reverses   Videotape of a reporter asking an interview subject a question. Usually shot over the shoulder of the interview subject after the interview is finished, so the question can be edited to an answer already videotaped. Can distort a TV story if the question is not worded and spoken exactly as it was when the answer was given. Another way to avoid a jump cut. See Chapter 4.

Sig Out   The close of a reporter "package" or "wrap" in which the reporter signs out. "I'm Earl Egotist, Channel 14 Action News." See Chapters 1 and 6.

Share The percentage of households watching television who are watching a specific program at any given time. A share is that station or network's share of the audience actually watching TV. A show's rating is the percentage of households who own a TV set in the market area who are watching at a specific time. See Chapter 6.

Shotgun Mike An elongated, directional microphone which can be pointed at a person and pick up conversation at a greater distance than the ordinary mike. Often used by TV crews where there is a large crowd and they are not able to get close to the person talking.

Sony Sandwich TV term for a reporter "package" or "wrap." At some stations, the Sony Sandwich is used to denote only live shots, in which the reporter speaks, then interviews someone, then closes the story. The interview, or videotape used in the middle of a live shot is the meat in the Sony Sandwich, and the reporter introduction and close, the bread. See Chapters 1 and 2.

SOT Short for Sound-on-Tape. Used in a script to tell the editor both the audio and video are on the same section of videotape. See Chapters 1 and 4.

Sound Bite A short portion of a videotaped interview which is edited into the reporter's story. Frequently shortened in TV jargon to "bite." See Bite and Chapter 4.

Squeeze Zoom An electronic device that enables the director to insert a videotape or live picture in a small area of the screen, then zoom it out to fill the entire screen, or vice versa.

Super Writing which is superimposed over video

during a broadcast. The name of the reporter or interview subject is supered when we first see them, to tell us who they are. A super saves time. The person appearing on camera does not have to be introduced.

Standup   A reporter's narration where we hear and see the reporter talking. Whether the reporter is standing, sitting, talking, driving or lying down, it's still a standup. See Chapters 1 and 4.

Sweeps   Four standard rating periods in which TV audiences are measured, and on which advertising rates are based. See Chapter 6.

Talent   TV talk for those staffers who are seen on TV. Reporters, anchors, sportscasters and weather forecasters are "talent."

Talking Head   Just what it says. Someone talking on camera with nothing to break the visual monotony.

Tap   Short for wiretap. See Chapter 11.

TelePrompTer   The device which projects a script on a pane of glass in front of a studio camera, allowing the anchor to read it while he appears to be looking directly into the camera lens. See Chapter 1.

Tight Shot   A closeup or telephoto shot, where the scene or person appears to be very close to the camera. A tight shot of a person might fill the TV screen with just the face.

Two-Shot   A picture that includes two people, usually the reporter and the interview subject. Also used when two people are on camera at the same time in a TV studio.

UHF   Ultra High Frequency TV band. Channels 14 and higher.

VCR Short for videocassette recorder.

VHF Very High Frequency TV band. Channels 2 through 13.

Video The picture you see on TV, as distinguished from audio – what you hear. Video and audio are carried on separate tracks of videotape. During the editing process, the audio that originally was recorded when the tape was shot can be replaced with other audio, or mixed with it. The most common mixing involves editing a reporter's voice over the natural sound on the shooting tape, so we can hear, in the background, what was going on when the tape was shot. See Chapter 4.

Voice-Over This can be done live, or edited onto videotape. We hear the voice of the reporter or anchor while we see video – usually what the narrator is talking about. On videotape, the reporter's voice is mixed with the original sound on the tape, which we can still hear in the background. In live voice-over, the sound on the tape is turned down. We can hear that sound *under* the voice of the anchor, who is talking *over* the sound on the tape. See Chapter 4.

V/O-SOT Shorthand for a TV story formula. Voice-over to sound-on-tape. The anchor reads, V/O while we see video of what he is talking about. Then the anchor stops reading and we hear and see a videotaped interview – SOT. See Chapter 4.

Voting The process where viewers in a ratings sample cheat and log a favorite program in their daily diaries, even if they didn't watch it. Viewers in rating samples also are inclined to vote for cultural or educational programs when they were actually watching wrestling or sit-com reruns. See Chapter 6.

VTR Short for videotape recording. Is gradually being replaced in the jargon by VCR. Video-tape recorders were originally reel-to-reel machines, and the VTR term was created. Most videotape cameras now used in the field use videocassettes, and TV news people are switching to VCR when they talk about videotape recorders.

Wide Shot A wide-angle camera shot, showing a broad area. A wide shot in an office would show half the room. A tight shot would fill the screen with the face of the person being interviewed.

Wireless Short for wireless microphone. This is a small microphone and radio transmitter frequently used to pick up a reporter's voice or natural sound, and transmit it to a receiver, where it is then broadcast or recorded simultaneously with the video. Referees in sporting events wear wireless mikes so the audience can hear their calls. Reporters on the floor of a political convention use wireless mikes. Their picture is sometimes being shot by a camera halfway across the convention hall. The wireless enables them to talk to the camera without running a wire there. A wireless is legal so long as those in range of the microphone are aware it is transmitting their voices. A hidden wire-less, secretly transmitting conversation, be-comes a "bug." See Bug and Chapter 11.

Wiretap A physical connection to a wire that secretly intercepts information carried on that wire. Usually a telephone line. Always illegal for pri-vate citizens, under both federal and state laws. Law enforcement agencies are allowed to wiretap under court authorization that lets them search for conversation that might be evidence of a crime. Sometimes called a tap. Pickups that use inductance microphones are technically not a wiretap. Legal in some states, illegal in others. See Chapter 11.

Wrap TV term for a reporter story that includes a videotaped interview. The interview is wrapped inside a reporter introduction at the beginning of the story, and a reporter conclusion after the interview. In some places, called a "package" or a "Sony Sandwich." See Chapters 1 and 2.

Zoom lens A lens with a variable focal length that allows it to zoom from a wide shot to a tight shot, or vice versa. When the camera appears to be moving in close the photographer is actually "zooming in." The camera remains stationary, as the lens gradually swings from wide-angle to telephoto.